A Little Book about Requirements and User Stories

Heuristics for requirements in an agile world

Allan Kelly

A Little Book about Requirements and User Stories

Heuristics for requirements in an agile world

Allan Kelly

ISBN 978-0-9933250-6-9

Leanpub

This is a Leanpub book. Leanpub empowers authors and publishers with the Lean Publishing process. Lean Publishing is the act of publishing an in-progress ebook using lightweight tools and many iterations to get reader feedback, pivot until you have the right book and build traction once you do.

Also By Allan Kelly

Xanpan

Xanpan appendix - Management and team

Agile Reader

Project Myopia

Continuous Digital

Contents

CONTENTS

About the author

Allan inspires digital teams to effectively deliver better products through Agile technologies. These approaches shorten lead times, improve predictability, increase value, improve quality and reduce risk. Most of his work is with innovative teams, smaller companies - including scale-ups; he specialises in product development and engineering. He uses a mix of experiential training and ongoing consulting. When he is not with clients he writes far too much.

He wrote his first program at the age of 12 on a Sinclair ZX81, in Basic. He quickly progressed and spent the mid-80's programming the BBC Micro in BBC Basic, 6502 Assembler, Pascal and Forth. As well as appearing in several hobbyist magazines of the time, he was a regular on BBC Telesoftware, with programs such as Printer Dump Program (PDP and PDR), Eclipse, Snapshot, Echos, Fonts, FEMCOMS and, with David Halligan, Demon's Tomb, and EMACS (Envelop Manipulation and Control System, nothing to do with its more famous namesake!).

Allan is the originator of Retrospective Dialogue Sheets[1], the author of several books including: "Xanpan - team centric Agile Software Development" and "Business Patterns for Software Developers", and a regular conference speaker.

Contact: allan@allankelly.net

---

[1]http://www.dialoguesheets.com/

i

Twitter: @allankellynet[2]

Web: http://www.allankelly.net/[3]

Blog: http://blog.allankelly.net/[4]

Also by Allan Kelly

Xanpan: Team Centric Agile Software Development

Ebook: https://leanpub.com/xanpan[5]

Print on demand: Lulu.com[6]

And your local Amazon[7]

Business Patterns for Software Developers

Published by John Wiley & Sons

Available in all good bookshops and at Amazon[8]

---

[2]https://twitter.com/allankellynet
[3]http://www.allankelly.net/
[4]http://blog.allankellynet/
[5]https://leanpub.com/xanpan
[6]http://www.lulu.com/shop/allan-kelly/xanpan-team-centric-agile-software-development/paperback/product-22271338.html
[7]https://www.amazon.com/s/ref=nb_sb_noss?url=search-alias%3Daps&field-keywords=Xanpan
[8]https://www.amazon.com/Business-Patterns-Software-Developers-Allan-ebook/dp/B007U2ZT7K

Changing Software Development: Learning to Be Agile

Available in all good bookshops and at Amazon[9]

---

[9]https://www.amazon.com/Changing-Software-Development-Learning-Become/dp/047051504X

1. Conversation and benefit

User stories are probably the most widely used requirements technique in the agile world. This humble little who-what-why template was originally devised in 2001 by a team at Connextra in London, and it quickly gained widespread adoption:

> As a someone I want to do something So that some result or benefit

Simple, really.

Many traditional requirements engineering and elicitation techniques are still valid in agile; it's just the results don't end up in a big document. Agile emphasizes just-in-time requirements rather than upfront preparation. The requirements person—be it the product owner, business analyst, product manager, or someone else—embodies the understanding of what is needed, and the user story represents the work that needs doing.

User stories have three attributes that fit well within agile:

- Lightweight: They don't impose a lot of (upfront) costs on the team
- Easy to understand: You don't need a five-day course to understand them

- Easy to share: Objectives are simple to communicate between the technical team and customers

It is the third of these attributes that makes user stories my preferred choice: they are inclusive. Customers can engage with stories. Many other techniques are superior in terms of analysis, rigor, and completeness. But these advantages come at a significant cost: They create a barrier between those skilled in the approach (technical experts) and those who are not (customers.) Because user stories are so simple, they help create common understanding.

(Thanks to Rachel for sharing.)

A Placeholder for a Conversation

User stories are not, and should not be, complete requirements for software development. People call user stories a placeholder for a conversation, meaning the stories capture the essence of what is wanted, but they don't contain the detail. When the time comes to do the work, there will be a discussion about what the stories need.

I think of stories as tokens for work to be done. They are not the work itself—that has not yet been defined—but they represent the work. These tokens can be prioritized, shuffled, refined, changed, split, and more. When a token rises to the top of the pile, it is time to work on the story.

The first job is to understand what the job is. Conversations about stories are not just between the requirements person and the coder. If the team contains software testers, include them, too. Indeed, having the tester in the conversation is more important than having the coder.

User stories themselves need not be perfect; in fact, the biggest mistake with user stories is trying to make them exactly that. They should be transitory and short-lived: a means to an end, not the end itself.

When it is time to have that conversation, try conducting it in person instead of through documentation. Written documents are more expensive than commonly recognized. Each document costs twice: writing time plus reading time. There are other more effective, more efficient forms of communication.

Having a conversation about a piece of work can be cheaper, timelier, and more effective than communicating via documents or email. In a conversation, people can ask questions, skip a section, or discuss a section in depth. So, save time (and money) by talking instead of writing documents.

Each Story Has Business Benefit

Each story should have some business value. The story may earn revenue, reduce costs, attract customers, make employees more effective, or deliver value in some other way. Putting a value on a story may require sales projections or an understanding of time savings. Ideally, I'd like to see a financial amount on each story— a hard dollar number that states the monetary value of the story. Having a financial value on a story makes prioritization easy.

I encourage teams to estimate story value in the same way some teams estimate work effort: with poker cards. Sometimes I'll invoke the TV show Shark Tank or Dragon's Den and have one team pitch its stories to another team. The other team plays investors and tries to assign value to the story.

However, putting a number value on a story can be hard, and not just because estimating a value can be hard. Sometimes stories aren't quantifiable because they deliver something intangible, or because one story delivers a small piece of something much bigger. Some stories improve the user experience, some improve quality, and others are given as unquestionable mandates: "This story simply has to be done."

Even if a story doesn't have a quantifiable benefit, it should have some statement of benefit. I like to see at least a short sentence with the story, saying something like:

"Fred says this story is beneficial because...."

Business benefit is anything that helps the business and business representatives accept the story as useful. might include learning and knowledge creation, enquiries into the market, and demonstrating commitment to a single stakeholder.

Someone, somewhere wants the story, and they should be able to express the reason as a benefit. If there is no identifiable benefit, then why build it?

User stories are far from perfect. But if I may borrow from Winston Churchill, I have come to believe that user stories are the worst requirements technique, except for all the rest.

2. Small and beneficial

I have two golden rules for user stories. The first is that each story should be beneficial to the business[1]. Ideally, it should carry a statement of value—of course, not all benefits have a financial value, so it is better to talk about *business benefit* than *business value.*

The second golden rule is: Each story should represent a small piece of work. While it's tough to define *how* small "small" is, basically, the piece of work should be deliverable sometime soon.

How small is small will depend on many things, as a rough rule of thumb small should mean less than two weeks elapsed effort. That is, from accepting a story for development until it be ready for delivery is less than two weeks (14 days, 10 working days) should pass. Although I'm generous, I know people who think two days is a long time.

Of course there are exceptions but they should be exceptions. Indeed, I would hope that most stories end up delivered a good deal sooner than two weeks. Always strive for smaller stories.

Bigger stories need to be broken down into smaller ones. However stories do not break themselves down. It takes work, if you don't try and make your stories smaller nobody else is going to.

---

[1] http://www.agileconnection.com/article/user-story-heuristics-understanding-agile-requirements

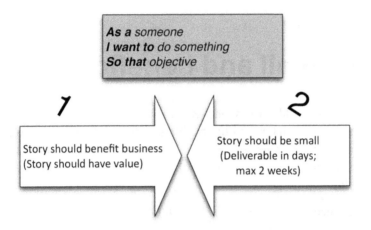

Two golden rules push against each other

A Balancing Act

There is tension between these two golden rules, and they often push in opposite directions. Getting stories that both exhibit business benefit and are small is difficult. The first golden rule of business benefit tends to push stories toward being larger, while the second golden rule that stories should be small tends to push stories toward being, well, smaller.

In the effort to make stories smaller, many stories lose their business benefit. When stories lose identifiable benefit, the business representatives lose interest in the stories—and in the work in general. This can also result in the technical team risk losing credibility.

When a product owner or other customer representative is part of story management and prioritization, he or she has the last say in what has benefit and what does not. Even if the technical team can see a way of breaking a story down into two independent chunks, if the requirements specialist cannot see benefit in each chunk, then the chunks do not have value and should not be split.

I know a team who split a story to preserve the system state into "Save data" and "Load data" stories. This makes sense from a technical point of view because each is an independent piece of work. But the business analyst said, "Neither has value on its own; only the whole has value to us." Thus, the stories did not stand as good stories. The technical team is within their rights to split the "Store and restore system state" story into one "Save data" task and a second "Load data" task and then implement them, but they should not be made into separate stories.

The technical team could engage in discussion with the business analysts and point out that simply being able to demonstrate the system saving the data could have business benefit, by showing progress to a customer. But the business analysts have the right to stick to their original position.

How Small Is "Small"?

How small is "small" will depend on many things, but as a rough rule of thumb, "small" should mean less than two weeks' elapsed effort—that is, from accepting a story for development until it is ready for delivery should take less than two weeks (ten workdays). This may be a generous definition; I know people who think two *days* is a long time.

Of course, there are exceptions, but they *should* be exceptions.

Indeed, I would hope that most stories end up delivered a good deal sooner than two weeks.

However, the goal is to always strive for smaller stories. In terms of process, this is preferable because smaller pieces of work flow through a process more easily. In terms of forecasting, it is better because smaller requests can be accomplished more quickly, which results in a smoother flow and greater predictability.

Business benefit increases because delivering work sooner generates benefit sooner, so the return on investment is greater.

With smaller individual stories, it is also easier to spot risks and identify troublesome work. Risk is further reduced because when work is flowing smoothly, the system as a whole is less prone to disruption.

Finally, the impact of encountering a problem is less because the affected work is smaller. Failure of a hundred-thousand-dollar piece of work costs a hundred thousand dollars, but failure of one of ten ten-thousand-dollar pieces of work of work is only ten thousand dollars.

So, What's the Right Size?

Unfortunately, there is no one right size for every user story. The size of a story depends on a number of factors, and the right size for one team may be too big or too small for another team.

One reason is that the size depends on the knowledge the team creating the software has. A team who has been working in the same domain for a long time will instinctively understand a lot more than a team new to a domain. They will need less explanation of what needs doing, and they will know the language, domain, and context of the story.

I once knew an outsourced development team working for an airline. Few on the development team initially had experience in the travel industry at all, let alone the airline business. The lack of experience meant they needed more help from the customer team and lots of detail on stories, and the stories were so small that it was difficult to see the business benefit.

Contrast this with a team who has worked directly for an airline for years. Faced with the same user story, this team will immediately know the industry terms and language, plus many of the airline's existing standards for things like passenger name length, punctuation, and more. Such a team can work with less detail and bigger stories.

Story size will also vary depending on the technologies in use. It appears that teams working in the more modern, high-level languages, such as PHP, Python, and Ruby, can handle bigger stories than those working in older system languages such as C, C++, and Java.

Iteration length and overflow rules will also play a role. Teams working on four-week iterations will be more willing to accept bigger stories, while those working on one-week iteration will challenge bigger stories more often. Given the advantages of small stories, the pressure created by shorter iterations can be beneficial.

Practice Makes Progress

Writing stories that are both small and beneficial is hard. It takes skill and practice, and it doesn't happen overnight or by attending a training course. (It won't even happen just because you read this article.)

Therefore, especially for people who are new to writing stories, every opportunity should be taken to make stories smaller. You will make some mistakes, but those mistakes will help you learn. Just don't lose sight of the goal of keeping stories small and tasks manageable—while retaining business benefit.

One day you may have too many small stories, when that happen it is time to start thinking about merging stories and making them bigger. Until then keep making them smaller - while retaining business benefit!

3. Assessing the Business Value of Agile User Stories

Some years ago I worked with an airline that was writing some new booking pages for its website. Following good practice, the airline's team tested the pages with sample users to see what they thought of the new design. On the whole the feedback was good, except one thing: The sample group of customers said the new pages made it harder to find the lowest price for a flight. The airline decided to go ahead with the new content anyway.

When the pages went live the airline's revenue went up. Customers were spending more money. What customers valued and what the airline valued were different things, there was no right or wrong.

Ideally, I'd like to see companies put a dollar amount on each planned business story, but to be fair, pinning down the financial value can be hard—especially in a corporate IT setting. And as this airline example highlights, it is not just a question of how much value is anticipated, but also how sustainable it is. One could argue that while the airline increased revenue in the short term, in time, customers would start to consider their flights more expensive and take their business elsewhere.

I want to look at ways to assess business value and some of the considerations to think about.

Calculating Business Value

The obvious way to put a business value on an agile user story is to consider what difference it will make and what financial benefit that will bring. Typically, we would expect new technology to either increase revenue or reduce costs.

Let's consider the following story:

> As a widget seller, I would like to sell my widgets online.

That might look easy, but some analysis is needed. For a start, how many widgets might we expect to sell online? That requires us to ask, do people buy widgets online? And if the answer is no, we need to ask, would people buy widgets online?

Once we get through these questions, suppose we determine that a hundred thousand people might buy widgets online. Then we need to ask what the selling price is likely to be. We might know what a widget sells for in a shop, but would people expect to pay less online?

When we eventually reach a figure, that breeds more questions, such as: If we sell widgets online, will we lose offline sales? This known as *cannibalization*: when one product or channel takes sales from another of your products or channels.

Answering these questions may well involve some guesswork, but herein lies another problem: Guesswork is open to questioning. If someone doesn't like your answer, they can attack the guesses you made to get to it.

The more background research and analysis you do, the less guesswork will be required, but eliminating guesses actually might not make calculations more accurate. In some cases, intuition and rough rules of thumb can be more accurate than complex formula and data. (Gerd Gigerenzer's book *Risk Savvy*[1] contains many such examples.)

If you get lucky, then as you do the analysis, you'll discover some driving forces that render all the others insignificant. For example, if in analyzing online and offline widget sales you were to find that over the last five years online sales were rocketing while offline sales were plummeting, then it becomes clear the future is selling widgets online.

Assessing Cost Savings

Making a rational assessment of the cost savings in an organization should follow a similar structure to the revenue example:

> As a supermarket manager, I want self-checkout lines so that I can reduce the number of cashiers.

Faced with such a story, we need to ask, how many customers will use the self-checkout? And how many cashiers might that replace?

One might also consider whether self-checkout might lead to increased theft or reduced opportunities to upsell additional products.

---

[1] http://www.economist.com/blogs/prospero/2014/05/qa-gerd-gigerenzer

Some of the same catches apply, generating the need for more guesses or further research. However, in situations like this, additional questions also come into play: Will the customer experience be better or worse? Such a qualitative change is even more difficult to value. Creating a worse shopping experience may not immediately affect the bottom line, but over time it can make a big difference.

A second question to ask is, how quickly will these changes happen? It might take years before customers are happy to use the self-checkout regularly and the staff can be reduced. Researchers have found cases where IT changes took decades to realize cost savings.

Time as a Business Factor

Time plays a still more insidious role in these calculations: The more analysis and research you do in order to tighten up your business case, the longer it takes, and time is money.

Initially, analysis and research costs money because someone gets paid to do it. It may also entail extra costs such as accessing research reports. But it also costs because such analysis and research delays development and release of a product into the market. Delaying product release means the benefits are delayed, too. Delay also leaves opportunities for competitors to release a product.

Back when new IT systems took months or years to develop— think about the days of COBOL and C programs—it made sense to do lots of upfront analysis. However, in a world of tools and frameworks with far higher productivity, such as Ruby on Rails and Amazon Web Services, it might be possible to develop a product, deploy it, and analyze the results in less time than it would take to do a detailed analysis.

The Importance of a Company Strategy

Answering some of the questions outlined here requires referencing your company's overall strategy, and perhaps the specific IT strategy. This provides one shortcut to evaluating user story requests: Does a story align with the business and technology strategy of the company? If not, you've saved yourself some analysis time.

However, this requires that companies have a strategy and that it is clearly communicated. Let me leave you with a story with three possible endings:

> As a taxi company, I want customers to be able to book a taxi using a phone app so that …

> a) I can reduce the number of people employed answering phones to save money.

> b) I can take more bookings for more taxis and generate more revenue.

> c) I can disrupt the business model of taxi companies and build a single global company.

Valuation of a story is going to be vastly different depending on which ending your story has, and the ending depends on your company strategy.

When presented with a new user story, these are all some major factors that should be considered when evaluating the important question of business value.

4. As a Who?

User stories are probably the most widely employed require-ments-gathering tool in agile software development. The user story captures a description of a software feature from an end-user perspective by describing the type of user, what the user wants, and why:

> As a *someone,* I want to *do something* so that *some result or benefit.*

I want to look more closely at the start of the user story. Namely, I want to talk about who that "someone" is.

One of my clients writes software for medical treatment. Like just about every other team, their initial stories began, "As a user, I want ..." After awhile, they started to write stories for more specific roles, such as "As a doctor" and "As a lab technician." A little later, they started writing stories about the ultimate customer: "As a patient, I want ..."

Improving their understanding of who used the software led them to see multiple products where previously, there was one. Identifying dedicated products helped them prioritize and accelerate delivery.

"As a User"? You Can Do Better!

Too many user stories begin,

> As a user ...

These words add nothing to the story. If you see them, delete them. Users are not homogenous. A minor improvement over this is

> As a customer ...

A customer is a more specific user, but again, they are not homogenous. When I see stories that start "As a user" or "As a customer," I can't help thinking that they were written in a hurry and little thought was given to who will actually work with the system.

Always seek to be as specific as possible about the *who* in a story, rather than targeting a generic "customer".

Roles, Personas, and Stakeholders

User stories are normally written about roles—the people who would use the system and actually put their hands on the keyboard (or perhaps the touch screen.) As a result, user stories not only lend themselves to a user-centric design paradigm, they encourage one—even when it is not applicable.

Some teams create personas to understand who will use the system. Personas are good; they originated in marketing and were adopted by the user experience design community. Personas bring texture, feeling, and an understanding of your target user. The combination of the words on the story and the persona help teams imagine and empathize with customers.

Personas also narrow the definition of who will use the system and help make the story smaller. But sometimes, it is helpful to go in the opposite direction: to stakeholders.

All personas play a role, and all roles are stakeholders, but not all stakeholders are roles. Stakeholders might have a direct requirement, or they may constrain the system—if that's the case, write stories that refer to stakeholders.

Stakeholders are individuals, or groups, who have an interest in the system. They might not benefit, indeed they may be advisedly effected by the system but still they have an interest.

Some stakeholders will never touch the system. For example, a call center manager may never use call-handling software, but he is a stakeholder. His staff will use the system, and as a result he may have requirements for the system, so you should write stories about him:

> As a call center manager, I want new employees to be able to learn to use the system in less than two days so that they are productive as soon as possible.

Unfortunately, because a stakeholder is more generalized than a role or persona, such stories may be larger in size. Watch for this and seek opportunities to redress the balance.

Spending time to identify stakeholders and user roles and create personas starts to add analysis to user stories. Some analysis is useful, but be careful to avoid analysis becoming an end in its own right. While a brief period of analysis can be helpful before development begins, diminishing returns quickly set in. Actually doing some work and looking at the results quickly becomes a faster way to learn.

Don't Write Stories about the Team

Development team members are not usually typical customers of
the software they create, so it rarely makes sense to write stories
about programmers, testers, analysts, managers, and others who
work on the team. Stories written about team members tend to
have a certain "make work" sound to them:

> As a programmer, I would like to write some code
> so that I can get paid for coding.

Sometimes teams fall into the trap of writing stories because
there is no defined end-user, customer, or beneficiary. The product owner in particular seems to suffer:

> As a product owner, I want the system to take
> payment from customers so that they can pay for
> their purchases.

While the product owner will certainly want customers to pay
for their purchases, the product owner is not the ultimate beneficiary; he or she is a proxy for the customer. This story would
be better written as:

> As a buyer, I want to pay for my purchases.

Even if the product owner were in some way the ultimate
beneficiary, this version of the story is shorter and clearer. (By
the way, if the *so that* clause is obvious or trivial—as it would

have been in the last example, as in, "so that I legally own them"—you can skip it.)

If stories are repeatedly written about team members, it may well be a sign that the product owner and team do not really understand who the customer is, who will use the product, and who will receive the benefits of the system. The product owner may be missing or not doing the job correctly.

Similarly, stories about organization entities show a lack of focus and understanding:

> As the business, I want lots of rich content so that search engines will index the site and bring visitors.

> As an online shop, we want customers to pay for purchases so that we have some revenue.

> As an airline, I want all flight options presented to searchers so that they can book a ticket.

Even leaving aside the grammatical and philosophical problems, it should be clear that each of these stories is vague and overly verbose. All these stories could be rewritten from a customer perspective. In doing so you might end up with more stories but these would be more specific and therefore potentially smaller. For example:

> As a business traveller I want options presented so I can book a flight which best fits my schedule

```
As a Mum I want to see which flights I can book for m\
y family of four during the summer so that I can trav\
el on the cheapest dates
```

Like other heuristics presented here, there are occasional excep-tions. Perhaps the best example of breaking this rule comes from testers:

> As a tester, I want to see a log of all user actions so that I can check that the final reports are what was requested.

Such extra functionality allows the team to work more effec-tively. Still, if there are many stories using this formula, then some questions need answering. Indeed, I consider any story that references the team or the organization building the software with suspicion. Explain the exception or rewrite the story.

Are systems roles?

One question that comes up often when I talk about roles in user stories is:

> "Can you have another system as a role?"

That is, if there is another system which needs to interface to yours, either as a data source or a data destination, should you cast a system as a role in a user story?

Such stories might be something like:

As the payroll system I want to know the tax code of every employee so I can calculate the income tax payments each month

As the ticketing system I want to know who has bought tickets so I can issue tickets to customers

On the one hand the other system plays a role, it has a part in the work of the system under development. On the other hand they aren't a user in the usual sense. Such stories reflect the way things are in organizations whether one likes it or not. One system imposes a demand on another. But is that the best way to work?

Lets take a step back and remember the mantra of user stories: *User stories are a placeholder for a conversation.*

Faced with a story like:

As the payroll system I want to know the tax code of every employee so I can calculate the income tax payments each month

Who are you going to have the conversation with? The payroll system developers might, or might not, be able to furnish you with documentation for data formats but when questions arise about the using the system(s) there is nobody to have a conversation with. One problem with computers system is that they are hard to negotiate with.

The lack of a human in the story leads to the next problem: how can you judge the benefit of a story before implementing it? Or evaluate benefit when work is complete? Again there is nobody to have a conversation with.

If you stop and think about it there is someone who will receive the benefit of system stories but they are not a system. Somebody, somewhere, will receive the benefit of these two systems collaborating - and if there isn't such a person then why are you doing the story?

Actually it is the result of two systems working together that someone has asked for. The story in question is actually one part of a bigger story which has been prematurely broken down. Sticking with the payroll example, there is actually a bigger story in play:

> As a payroll manager I want salary payments to made after tax deductions so that employees have simpler tax schedules

The real story requires two pieces of work in different systems: work in the system that holds employee tax codes and work in the payroll system. Now there is someone who will receive the benefit and that someone can answer questions and discuss requirements in detail. Quite possibly this stakeholder doesn't care which system does the work, or how the systems share the work, as long as the result is the same.

When faced with the temptation to write a story about a system step back, imagine the two systems (the one you are developing and the one you want to write a story about) as one system. Now ask: who wants this? who will use this? who will receive the benefit? Those questions will lead you to a somebody.

Once you have your bigger story it may well be that two teams - one for each system - need to coordinate their work together. The same story might exist in both backlogs but the work involved will be different. Provided such a story exists then I'm happy to see the occasional (smaller) story that talks of another system. Of course, if such stories start to proliferate it is probably a sign of trouble, one system story is OK, six is potentially a problem.

A better solution is to have one story for one team and allow the team to work on both systems. Remember stories should be vertical, end-to-end functionality, that implies the teams that code the stories need to be vertical too. Such teams need the skills and authority to work on both systems. Needing to split a story across two teams is not good, unfortunately it happens.

Conversation forgives and resolves

Better-written stories always help, but if conversations happen around the user stories—as they should—talking should resolve confusion. When conversations don't happen, greater demands are made of stories and they start to resemble requirements of old. If you find yourself arguing over the words on the card, then you probably aren't having the constructive conversation you want.

5. Stories, Epics, and Tasks

Making user stories small is hard. I recently ran a story-writing session with a team and their clients. We brainstormed a dozen stories and then prioritized them. We took the top one and talked about how we could make it smaller and simpler. I knew little about the system and the background, so I asked some obvious questions and challenged everything. I bet I was a pain.

The first cut started with an *and*. The card said "real time and historical reports." Whenever you see *and, or, either*, or *but*, look to split the card.

Fortunately, everyone in this meeting was open to splitting the stories. After awhile we had a multitude of stories derived from the first one.

Stories up and down

Some teams only work with stories. Their stories make sense to the business and to the technical team, are deliverable quickly— a few days at most—and have value. This is probably the ideal situation, but it doesn't work every time, and it can be difficult when a team is new to agile.

An alternative is to add epics and tasks. An epic is some big piece of functionality the business wants that is delivered via multiple smaller stories. Epics, by definition, break the rule that stories must be small, but they have the most business benefit. Tasks are smaller work items that build a story. They usually can be accomplished in a day or so, but by themselves they are devoid of business benefit.

Go Large with Epics

Sometimes, the business doesn't want something small; it wants something big! Indeed, it might want more than one big thing. An epic might represent a milestone or notable delivery, or an epic can be a placeholder, something to break down into smaller pieces in future.

It makes sense to use the user story "As a ..." format for epics, but there is no law that says you must. Just remember that *who*, *what*, and *why* are useful things to know.

Go Small with Tasks

On the other hand, it sometimes makes sense to break a story down into the work that needs to be done. In calling out the tasks needed to build a story, the development team engages in an act of shared design. Tasks are not normally written in user story format. Instead, they are written by the team, for the team, so use language the team will understand.

A task is a piece of work that needs doing, usually in order to build toward a bigger story. As such, it does not have independent deliverable functionality or generate business value, and, unlike a story, it normally is not a vertical (end-to-end) slice.

Most tasks tend to be for programmers, but they could be for testers, analysts or anyone else on the team.

Unlike stories tasks don't have business value but they are small. Typically a task is a day or less, may be a few hours work or a couple of days at most. I even allow "zero point tasks" which are little more than placeholders for trivial work ("Call Bob and tell him the system is up") or to track work external to the team ("Bob to update database").

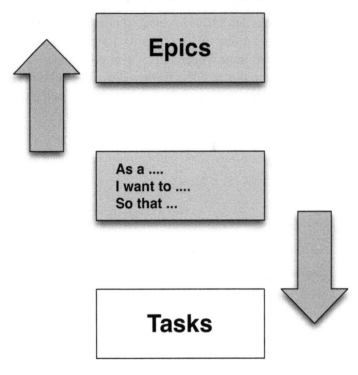

Epics have vale but are
too big to deliver soon

Epics

As a ....
I want to ....
So that ...

Tasks

Tasks are small enough to be
done really soon but lack their
business value by themselves

Up to Epics, down to tasks

Not all stories get broken down into tasks. Breaking a story down is an act of design, so whether a breakdown is required or not depends on existing knowledge, the technologies under development, the architecture, and, most of all, the size of the story to start with.

Tasks are useful because they allow the technical team to call out discrete pieces of work without pretending they mean something to the business. Having the whole team examine a story, especially when that brings different points of view, opens up the story. Different team members see different ways of breaking a story down, either as tasks or as smaller stories.

Three Organizational Levels

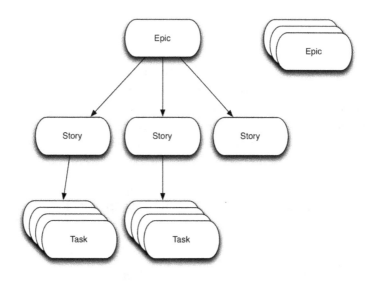

Figure 1: Three levels of stories

When I used to run teams, I found that two levels were enough: stories and tasks. However, I regularly meet teams who use epics and stories and seldom, if ever, do tasks. Just because there are multiple organizational levels, don't feel you have to use all three. If you only need two, good, and if you only need one, then better still.

Avoid the temptation to introduce more levels. Adding levels increases administration and gets more confusing. When you are using an electronic tool, hierarchies can get complicated quickly, and extra complications distract from the real goal. So avoid *tertiary epics, intermediate stories, subtasks,* and the other names given to additional layers. Whenever I see teams who have added to the hierarchy, the effort and complications introduced are greater than the benefit. If you feel the need to group several stories, remember that you can do this without a hierarchy. Paper clips work well!

That being said, epics and tasks sometimes go by other names, especially natively within tools. Tasks can be called *subtasks,* stories sometimes go by the name *features,* and epics can go by the name *themes.* Some teams like to organize their work around user activities, which may be stories, epics, or something else.

If your team, organization, or tool wants to use different language, that's fine; names are not important. Just ensure that your entire team understand what is meant by each term, use the terms consistently, and stick to three or fewer levels.

Color Coding and Planning

I like to code **tasks** by putting them on **white cards**. That makes obvious what they are. I use **blue cards** for **stories** — you might say "Blue is for business." I'll also use **blue for epics**, but epics seldom make it to the board. Epics are big things, and for a team working in the small, the focus should be on getting the small things done.

These three levels line up well with planning:

- White tasks are for now and the iteration that is about to happen, and they are mainly for the team.
- Blue stories are what the product owner is lining up for the near-term iterations.
- Epics are for the future: Epics touch on strategy and may even be beyond the product owner.

Making Use of Your Choices

Being able to choose among stories, epics, and tasks brings flexibility to an agile team, but don't think you must use epics and tasks. Sometimes when stories are decomposed into multiple smaller stories, each stands on its own and no hierarchy is needed. When a story is really small, knowing what needs doing can be trivial. Having a clear understanding of the differences between each level and knowing what size story to use for each situation will improve the accuracy of your sprint planning.

6. Defining Acceptance Criteria

Agile teams often employ user stories to organize project requirements. When using physical index cards to assemble requirements, teams use the backs of the cards to capture acceptance criteria — also called *conditions of satisfaction*, or just ACs. Acceptance criteria are the main points or general rules to consider when coding and testing the user story.

ACs are not acceptance tests. Professional testers can elaborate these criteria later to produce test scripts. Test scripts, whether automated or manual, are detailed and specific, and they certainly require more space then an index card!

As with the story on the front of the card, the finite amount of space on the back of the card limits writing. That is deliberate. Stories shouldn't contain every last detail—far from it. In elaborating the stories and writing the tests, coders and testers should continue having conversations with each other and the business representatives.

Teams using electronic systems may also record acceptance criteria there, but without the limits imposed by physical cards, these teams have to resist the temptation to add more and more detail. Remember: A story is a placeholder for a conversation. Resist the urge to get detailed in ACs.

Acceptance Criteria and Testers

ACs expand on the initial story, so they are usually written by the same person who wrote the original story—probably the business representative or product owner (PO). However, when a PO is short on time, ACs are frequently dropped. That is not *always* a bad thing, but it may well be the sign of a problem. Testers might need step in to add acceptance criteria themselves.

Usually, testers begin their work with existing ACs. They may give feedback to the PO on how to improve the criteria, but their main role is to take the ACs and create actual tests from them. Hopefully these tests are automated, but if not, they will be natural language descriptions of how to perform the tests.

If you don't have professional testers on the team then turning ACs into test might fall to the product owner. However this puts more work onto someone who probably has more than enough already. Sometimes developers might write tests themselves, this can be great, it can also be awful. It depends on the individuals and environment.

Even if there are no testers and the ACs aren't turned into fully fledged test they are still useful. They promote conversation between PO and developers and help both sides improve their understanding.

The story and ACs form the requirement; the tests form the specification. Requirements describe what the business wants to achieve, while specifications describe the detailed parameters within which the solution needs to perform. Specifications always need to be testable. Techniques such as *specification by example* and *acceptance test-driven development* make specifications themselves executable as automated tests. (More on this in the appendix.)

If it helps product owners to talk to testers or programmers when writing stories and acceptance criteria, then they should. And if it helps testers to write tests by talking to the programmers and POs, they also should. Teams that encourage such collaboration sometimes call these discussions "Three Amigos" or the "Power of Three." In these conversations, people representing requirements, testing, and coding come together to talk about the story. Not only will they discuss the story and ACs, but they also may change them, add to them, or split the story into multiple smaller stories.

The Level of Detail

Consider this example:

> As a delivery company, I want to have the customer's full postal address on packages so that I can deliver them correctly.

Such a story might have ACs like:

> Customers must provide a valid postal address

> Shipping labels must carry a correctly formatted address

Notice that a "valid postal address" is not defined. That kind of detail can be left until later, as ACs are not the place to elaborate. (An exception might be when some non-obvious detail is important, say, using all nine digits of the ZIP code.)

The amount of detail needed depends on the knowledge and experience of the programmers and testers. A tester might just use her existing knowledge to write the test script, or a programmer and tester may need to research what constitutes a "valid address." In this postal address scenario, a tester who is testing software for a country she has never visited might ask for more details than the product owner expects. If that's the case, there quickly comes a point where conversation between the product owner and tester would be better.

The Right Time to Define

I am frequently asked, "When should we write the acceptance criteria?" Sometimes programmers resist giving an effort estimate for a story unless they can see the ACs—sometimes detailed ACs, at that. However, there is little point in POs (and testers) spending time on ACs until stories are about to be scheduled. After all, if ACs take hours to write and the story is not scheduled, their time is wasted.

Also, suppose ACs are added but then the story doesn't get scheduled for a year, by that time the story and the ACs may have changed. Because old criteria are in place, it can be easy to overlook these potentially important changes. (And any effort estimate is similarly out of date.)

I would rather product owners did not write ACs until the last possible moment—even just before the planning meeting - think of it as *just in time acceptance criteria*. At that point they should be fairly sure what they will request from the team. This would have the beneficial effect of forcing brevity on the PO.

Writing ACs inside the iteration neatly sidesteps the problem of postponed or canceled work. This means the team must be prepared to accept—and even estimate, if needed—stories without ACs. Because writing ACs might well be the first task in an iteration before any code or tests are written, any effort estimates given must be for the work required to "write ACs and deliver the code" rather than just "deliver the code."

Another solution I have had some success with is writing the ACs within the planning meeting. At this point, teams know the stories to schedule. This will make the planning meeting longer, but on a small team there is unlikely to be many stories. A large team can split into smaller groups and work on stories separately.

Test scripts based on ACs are best created within the iteration, preferably before coding begins. Creating test scripts is part of the work of delivering a story.

Acceptance Criteria in Action

Acceptance criteria can be helpful in expanding on and elaborating user stories. However, ACs should not be seen as a substitute for a conversation; they are not a route back to long documents and extremely detailed requirements.

Remember to use ACs sparingly to record key criteria at a high level. Defer details to conversations within the iteration and elicit specifications as needed.

7. Acceptance Criteria, Specifications, and Tests

Back in the dark days before agile, a friend of mine, Tony, worked on a government project that trusted in upfront, written requirements and specifications. One day a screen Tony had developed failed testing because the specification stated that a "Please wait" icon should display while the system was accessing the database.

But database access happened very fast — far faster than the analyst who wrote the original request had considered. Rather than discuss the specification, it was easier for Tony to introduce a delay so that testers (and, later, users) could admire the hourglass icon before seeing the results.

The specification Tony faced might well exist in an agile world, only instead of being a line item in a boring document somewhere, it would be part of the acceptance criteria on a story. Because stories and acceptance criteria are placeholders for a conversation — not rigid mandates — having a conversation about those requests can resolve mismatches like what Tony experienced.

This conversation isn't necessarily a single event. It can, probably should, be an ongoing discussion as the testers and programmers work to build the story. As understanding improves, the story can, and will, change.

In an agile world, I would hope Tony's predicament never arises. The icon request was premature — an attempt to second-guess the future — and it created more work for the writer, the tester, and the developer. In an agile world, the next iteration could always be to add an icon if it's needed, so it is safe to postpone a decision and omit the criteria.

Even if the request did make it into the original acceptance criteria, then during the discussion about the story, Tony would get a chance to ask, "What if the database returns very quickly?" If the question wasn't asked beforehand, I would expect Tony, and perhaps the tester, to talk the issue through with the product owner. And I would expect the product owner to have the knowledge and authority to say, "There is no need to display a timer when the result is fast."

Splitting Stories by Acceptance Criteria

One of the things teams typically find difficult is making stories small. Getting pieces of work that then can be delivered in a few days and demonstrate business benefit is undoubtedly hard. And when you've not done it before, it's harder still!

Acceptance criteria, or ACs, have a role to play here. Each individual criterion is potentially a story in its own right.

Take the first AC, write it on the back of a new index card, and write a story on the front that contains some element of the original user story. Even if you need to restrict the story in some way, you may still have something that delivers a teeny-tiny bit of business benefit — something that shows progress or advances understanding and the conversation.

In the process, decoupling the work has reduced the risk of the original story. The risk is further reduced because you now have a tiny piece of functionality that demonstrates a bigger story: an even thinner vertical slice.

The new story comes before the original and provides small stepping stone on the way to something bigger. Take the next AC on the original card and repeat the processes for each AC. Some ACs may not lend themselves to this approach but at least try.

Specifications and Tests

In everyday conversation, IT folks use the terms *requirements* and *specifications* interchangeably, as if they mean the same thing. They don't.

- Requirements are the things the customers want to achieve; think of them as a problem for the team to solve.
- Specifications are the parameters within which the solution must operate. They are the details that can make crafting a solution hard.

Each one of your ACs will, in time, expand to one or more tests. Together, these form the specifications of the story. The front of the card spells out the requirement — the thing asked for — while the ACs and tests describe the exact parameters that define and constrain the work.

In other words, specifications are tests, and tests are specifications. After all, how can anyone know if the specification has been satisfied if it cannot pass a test? (If someone tells you they cannot give you acceptance criteria, tell them the work is complete and mark it as done. The resulting bug reports will provide the missing tests.)

Automating these tests and executing them by a machine creates *executable specifications*. In truth, even a manual test script is executable after a fashion, but that execution is slow, expensive, and error-prone.

Specification by Example

In creating your tests you need to generate some small amount of data, you need to come up with a test scenario. This itself is an example of what the system needs to do. Such examples can be useful beyond mere tests.

Users who don't know about technology can read these examples, comment on them, and discuss their correctness. Examples can even be mentally tested, if needed. This is *specification by example*. The example models the specification.

Rather than writing a dry set of rules that state "The system shall ..." and "The system must ..." an example gives a better illustration: "When I show the system a picture of a square, it displays square." This example is more interesting, and more accessible to a novice.

Models and examples have more useful attributes, too. You can take other examples and mentally compare them, and counterexamples can help to determine if the original represents existing functionality or something new. If it is something new, you can add it to the test set; it will fail at first, but then you know you have work to do.

Test Automation: More Than Fast

Specification by example and executable specifications are the key ideas underpinning behaviour driven development (BDD) and automated acceptance test-driven development (ATDD). More than automating tests, the real value of these techniques is in promoting meaningful conversations between different people in different roles with different experience.

Automating your tests makes them fast and cheap to execute, and many people think that is what test automation is all about. But is isn't.

Test automation is a game changer. Because test execution is fast, it provides feedback much sooner, so the feedback loop is tightened. Because test automation is rigorous — it's code! — it flushes out details and anomalies. Because test automation remains in place, it provides a legacy, a sort of insurance policy, which catches future problems.

Traditional tests written in verbose, boring English or a hiero-glyph programming language form a barrier to conversation. When users and customers can understand tests, they become powerful communication tools for enhancing learning and understanding on all sides.

Finally, readable tests form documentation, and because the tests are executable (and get executed regularly against actual code), there is no space or time for discrepancies between specification documentation, tests, and code. Specifications *are* tests, and test automation ensure than any variance between specification and code is quickly identified.

8. Definition of Done

Hang around teams working on agile projects and you'll frequently hear people talking about "done" and "done-done." What they mean is that work not only is completed, but also complies to the common standard known as the *definition of done*. The work is both "done" and "done" to an agreed set of criteria.

The definition of done is an informal checklist that the team agrees applies to all pieces of work. The whole team is responsible for approving and writing the definition of done and applying it to every story they work on.

When I say it's an informal checklist, I mean there is no paperwork or formal sign-off process associated with a definition of done. It is an aide memoir, a reminder, and an agreement among team members that before anyone attempts to mark a story as done, it will pass all the points on the checklist.

One team I worked with had four items on the checklist:

- JUnit tests written for code
- Peer code review conducted
- Product owner approved
- Interface to third-party system double-checked

The team wrote this list on their team board, where it was clearly visible to everyone. Before any card moved to the *done* column, the team members would ask themselves: *Have I done these four things?*

Acceptance Criteria or Definition of Done?

Teams sometimes get confused between the definition of done and acceptance criteria, or they worry about the interplay between these two completion tests.

A definition of done is not an alternative to the acceptance criteria; it is a generic baseline for all stories. Each story brings its own special acceptance criteria. In effect, every set of acceptance criteria has an unwritten first item: "Conforms to the definition of done."

Or, to put the other way around, every definition of done has as a implicit line item: "All acceptance criteria pass."

Perhaps surprisingly, I frequently meet team members who do not agree on what constitutes *done*! For example, one developer will only push a card to done after a code review, while another will not even ask for a code review. Without a general agreement on what *done* means, how can a team ever hope to be consistent?

This is where a definition of done helps. This isn't something imposed from outside or above; it is important that the definition is the result of team involvement and agreement.

The aim of both acceptance criteria and the definition of done is to improve the quality of the code produced. Research — and programmer intuition — consistently shows that higher-quality code saves time and, therefore, money. When code is low-quality is must be repeatedly tested, fixed, retested, and fixed again. Time increases, costs escalate, and schedules disintegrate in the face of poor quality.

Task Twist

There is a twist on the definition of done for teams who break stories down to tasks. When teams break down work, the question arises: *Does the definition of done apply to stories or tasks?*

As long as the team agrees, the definition of done can apply to either or both. Take the four-line bulleted definition I gave above. If applied at a task level, then JUnit and code reviews work fine. If there was something to show the product owner on the task, then sure, the owner can see it and approve it, but if it was an internal change (e.g., a database schema change), that check would be trivial. Similarly, if the task didn't touch the third-party system, then there is nothing to check.

As long as the team talks through the various scenarios and comes to an agreement on how they will use the definition, then it should work. Again, the important thing is to have consistent understanding within the team.

I once met a team who went so far as to define two definitions of done: one for the task level and one for the story level. That might seem a bit over the top, but if the team thinks it helps and it doesn't add to the administration burden, then why not?

Similar logic applies at the epic level, but because epics exhibit more variability, it seldom seems to be necessary to apply a definition of done at the highest level. *Done* for an epic is frequently a more subjective judgment. I certainly would avoid saying "All stories complete" for any definition of done that applies to an epic. Such criteria can lead to teams building stories that aren't needed.

Working within Columns

A definition of done is normally, as the name implies, applied to work entering the final stage, namely, "done." For teams using a visual board to track work, this means work entering into the final column of the board. But it is also possible to extend the idea of the definition of done across the board.

Another way of thinking about the definition of done is that it represents the preconditions for work entering the *done* state. Because nothing occurs between the previous work-in-progress state (board column) and the done state, the definition also forms the post-condition, or exit criteria, of the previous state and board column.

From here, it is an obvious step to think about the exit criteria for each state. Each column on the board can have its own definition of done. Few teams are so rigorous as to write such a definition for every state, but teams will frequently have "Acceptance criteria completed" as an exit condition on an analysis column.

Reviewing and Updating the Definition

Finally, the definition is not set in stone. Teams should peri-odically — quarterly perhaps — take their definition of done and review every item. Over time, tightening the definition should lead to higher-quality code. Conversely, an overly long definition might be self-defeating, as people will eventually consciously or subconsciously skip steps.

In fact, given long enough, I would hope that the items listed in the definition become so normal and ingrained that people comply with the definition without even thinking about it. At that point, the definition becomes redundant; teams remove it to create an even lighter process, or they rewrite it with new items to encourage even better quality.

9. Working with Nonfunctional Requirements

Some years ago a bank asked me for advice on a project to change the processing of payments for Scandinavia. This was a small piece of work, and the bank wanted to use some agile goodness to speed up development — but they didn't want agile to disrupt anything else. Unfortunately, this is a common request: "Make us faster, but don't change anything."

Reviewing the requirements document — yes, they still had them — I asked, "How much time does this process have to operate in?"

"Oh, it runs in the early hours of the morning. The current process has a couple of hours to spare, so we are OK."

"Well," I responded, "let's put the current run time and the maximum time available into the specification. At least then we know what we have to work within."

This wasn't popular. "But then we would need to test it to see the current time. Setting up a test is going to take time, but the test system is already maxed out and we don't have any testers to do the test."

I gave up. There comes a point when persisting isn't going to help. But guess what? When put live, the new code functioned correctly, but it took so long to run that it hadn't finished when the bank opened for business.

Analysts call constraints like a limited time window *nonfunctional requirements*, or NFRs. (Personally, I think this is more a specification, but let's not get hung up.) The point is, there is a constraint that is independent of what functionality the system has. In this example, processing payments is well understood; the problem is whether it happens in one hour or four.

NFRs describe aspects of the system that do not map onto a single piece of functionality. Speed of execution is the most commonly cited NFR, but there are others. Ease of use is another common one, although how one measures ease is another question. Security is an increasingly common and important one, too.

Nonfunctional User Stories

Whether you see them right away or they appear as you discuss stories and acceptance criteria, you will inevitably have some NFRs.

With a little thought, regular user story format is fine for most NFRs:

> As an accounts clerk, I want the balance sheet report
> to be delivered within two minutes.

NFRs may appear within the story, as in this example or they may form part of the acceptance criteria on the back of a card. But not all NFRs are so easy. If your effort to twist a requirement into a user story leads you to break grammar rules or write convoluted sentences, then abandon the "As a..." user story format. Write requirements so they are understandable, and follow up with discussion later. You can still write acceptance criteria on the back if you wish.

Sometimes, especially when a system already exists, NFRs are just like any other piece of work. Take the balance sheet example: If the clerk can already obtain a balance sheet report, then the story is really saying, "Make the current functionality faster."

The key to NFRs is usually tests. In the first instance, a NFR is a request for testing. Before you do any development work, create and run the tests. Be truly test-driven.

Where functionality, does not currently exist then in the first instance there may be no work to do. The non-functional requirement represents a constraint on future work. In such cases the first job might be to developed the initial functionality. So start by splitting a story like the one above in two:

> As an accounts clerk, I want the balance sheet report.

> As an accounts clerk, I want the balance sheet report to be delivered within two minutes.

In the first story, you build the functionality; the second story necessitates a test that might create more work.

Once you have the tests in place, you will know whether any development work is necessary. Running the tests regularly ensures that any changes that break the requirement are quickly highlighted.

This is the catch with an NFR: Because they are cross-cutting, they can come back to bite you long after you consider them done.

One team I know had a performance requirement to return results in less than one second. First they created a test for this that passed; then they created a test that failed at 0.8 seconds. If this test broke in the future, they would soon need to take action to improve performance.

Specifying the Requirements

This approach demands quantifying NFRs: *How fast is fast? How secure is secure?*

This, in turn, means measurement tools. How do you measure *secure?* "The system can withstand a distributed denial of service attack for thirty minutes"?

It is useful here to borrow from the work of systems engineer and author Tom Gilb. He advocates using a "planguage" (planning language) based on well-defined rules for specification. He would ask:

- What is the unit of measurement? And what is the measuring tool?
- What is the current measurement?
- What is the desired measurement?

Perhaps the story answers these questions, or maybe the acceptance criteria do. If not, ask them in the conversation that follows. Without answers to these questions, tests, especially automated tests, become hard to create. Worse, NFRs become subjective — what is fast to me is not fast to you.

Constraints and Value

When you put tests in place for NFRs, it becomes clear that these items are not so much requirements as constraints:

As an accounts clerk, I want the balance sheet report to be delivered within two minutes.

NFRs provide parameters within which the system needs to operate, much like any other form of specification. Viewing requirements reveals they are not binary all-or-nothing requests. Rather than asking "Do we have function X or not?" ask "How much of this function do you need?"

Thinking like this makes all requirements analog — are they more satisfied or less satisfied?

- How fast does the balance sheet need producing?
- How accurate should the balance sheet be?
- How current should the balance sheet be?
- How are subsidiaries to be shown?

This gives us another tool with which to break stories down into smaller pieces. Rather than ask "Will feature X be developed?", ask instead "How much of feature X will be developed?" or "How close to constraints is the feature?"

More importantly, it also brings us back to benefit and value. How much value do these constraints produce? In effect, how much more valuable is it for the clerk to have the balance sheet in two minutes rather than four?

(Anyone familiar with Jeff Patton's ideas on story fidelity should see parallels.)

Knowing the value of functionality opens more doors. It helps perform cost-benefit analysis and allows consideration of different engineering solutions. How much value does producing a balance sheet in two minutes add? If the first story produces a balance sheet in four minutes, is there enough value to make the second story worthwhile?

Illuminating these constraints changes our understanding of the story and demands the conversation continues. Closing the conversation prematurely hides opportunities to split stories, negotiate compromises, and maximize benefits.

Opportunities to Benefit

Non-functional requirements lay out the parameters within which are system needs to operate. This is what engineering is all about! Engineers create solutions to problems within a set of constraints.

The real problem with constraints is not so much crafting a solution to meet them, but recognizing they are there in the first place. Creating tests and examples promotes conversations — a massive step toward flushing out nonfunctional requirements.

Applying the same logic to regular, functional, requirements has benefits too. It opens opportunities to further slice stories and consider benefit.

10. Stakeholders

Bill was a software development manager at a logistics company. One of his responsibilities was to decide what his team would develop next. There was no shortage of ideas; people would regularly come to him with requests to change or enhance one system or another. Usually, though, it was the account managers who got what they wanted, because they could link their requests back to customer revenue.

Bill had a varied bunch of stakeholders who all had an interest in the company systems, what his team was working on, and how his work would affect them, both directly and indirectly. Bill's answer was to step back and let his stakeholders prioritize the work.

Every two weeks Bill convened a meeting of the people who sent him requests. He put all the requests on the table and stepped back. The stakeholders would discuss the work requests among themselves and put them in priority order. At the end, Bill would get the result and set about delivery.

How they arrived at this priority is less important than the fact that they did. Those who could pin revenue to a story still stood a better chance of getting their request done, but those who couldn't put a financial figure on their story got a chance to argue their case, too.

Seeking Out the Real Benefit

Instead of choosing what to develop based solely on a cold, hard dollar amount, you might try approaching the person who originally requested the story and asking, "What benefit will this bring you?" or "What will X allow you to achieve that you can't at the moment?" An experienced business analyst may well be able to turn an answer like "This will allow us to reduce the time we spend answering customer calls" into a financial value.

You needn't have all stakeholders in the same room; you might not even want them to fight it out among themselves. But this way you can still get an understanding of the potential benefit of each proposed story.

You may also try talking to people other than those who originally requested the story; the potential new functionality could benefit different groups. Conversely, some stakeholders may actively *not* want changes made.

My friend Benjamin tells a story of receiving a stream for feature requests for his team. He made a point of tracking the requests back to the people who would receive the benefit, rather than the people who suggested the story. When he did so, he found the actual benefits could be negligible.

Stakeholder analysis — understanding who has an interest in a system under development, and what that interest is — is an old business analysis technique. Many tools and practices traditionally deployed by business analysts are still valid in today's agile world; analysts just need to accelerate the techniques for use in conjunction with development — days, not months, in advance.

Armed with a list of stakeholders and interests, you can find out the real difference a story will make. Having a statement that speaks to the business benefit can substitute for a financial valuation and is often a lot easier to obtain.

However, there are two potential downsides here. First, if story X has a value of a hundred thousand dollars put on it and story Y has a statement, not a value, then story X will probably get prioritized, even though it might not have the highest value. People tend to put more trust in numbers.

Second, those who don't agree with the valuation or who wish to fight for another story may endlessly ask for details of calculations and find fault. It's hard to argue against "making the numbers more accurate," but to do so can represent a diversion of time and energy, and it can be a distraction from actually getting on and doing the work.

Evaluation: Closing the Loop

However you go about evaluating your stories — by financial analyst, stakeholder analyst, or something else — there is one more step that is often lacking: Evaluation.

This should probably fall to the business analysts or product manager. After development and deployment, a story (or anything else) needs to be reviewed again to see if it delivered the expected result. Is the new functionality even used? Does it deliver the anticipated benefit?

If the benefit is not delivered, then why not? Maybe the benefit was wrongly identified or valued in the beginning, in which case development should never have worked on the story. Or maybe the work was insufficient, and the story just needs more work to realize the anticipated benefit.

Evaluating also allows teams to calibrate and adjust the current and new work to incorporate the findings from past work. It's just another feedback loop, but it's an important one, particularly in corporate IT settings.

If you follow this cycle - checking with those who will be affected by a story, ascertaining what benefits will be gained and then revisiting stories to evaluate whether the predicted benefit was realized - the you add another feedback loop. This in turn allows improvement to the story prioritization process and, ultimately, delivery of more stories that really matter.

11. Estimating Business Value

You know this TV show. The investors line up on one side of the room — a few more than usual — and the entrepreneurs line up on the other side. One, calling himself *the product owner*, steps forward and opens his pitch.

> "Our product is a website and app for food trucks. It allows food truck owners to find locations where they can park and sell food. They also can see what other competitors and cuisines there are at a location. For hungry customers, our app allows them to find a specific food truck's location or cuisine and read reviews of trucks."

No sooner has he finished than the investors start shooting questions at him: "How will you monetize the application? How many customers do you expect? Will it be available nationally? What about internationally? How will you ensure quality?"

Half the questions the product owner has ready answers for, but everyone can see he is improvising on others. As the questions slow, the host steps forward and hands each investor a set of cards. To most people these cards look funny but to software engineers, these cards are instantly recognizable: 0, 1, 2, 3, 5, 8, 13....

The host holds up an index card he took from the entrepreneurs earlier. "This," he says, "is your benchmark: one thousand American shillings. It's a new currency; I don't know the exchange rate right now, but we'll find out." He then reads from the card:

> "As a food truck operator, I want to see all the registered food trucks in my area on a map so I can decide where to park at lunchtime."

"Your cards," he tells the investors, "are denominated in thousands of American shillings." He holds up a poker card with the number 1 on it. "This card represents the thousand American shillings this story is worth." He writes "1,000 AS" on the card and sticks it on the wall.

The product owner reads from another index card:

> "As a food truck operator, I want to know how many hungry customers visited a location yesterday, last week, and last month so I can see where there are lots of customers."

Again the investors respond with a battery of questions, some technical, some business. After a few minutes the host moves the entrepreneurs to a vote. Each secretly selects a card to indicate the value they think the first user story has. "Three ... two ... one ... play 'em!" calls the host, and they show their cards. The host averages the values while the investors quiz each other. "Nine thousand American shillings," he announces, and writes "9,000 AS" on a card before pinning it to the wall above the first user story card.

The game plays on: The entrepreneurs pitch each user story, the investors query them, they vote on the value, and the host builds a list on the wall in value order. Sometimes the entrepreneurs write completely new stories as the conversation generates new ideas and immediately pitch them. Cards they had planned to pitch are discarded as new cards are written and they sense the investors interests.

At the end of the exercise there is a value-based priority list on the wall and a pile of discarded stories on the floor — and everyone has a much better understanding of what they are building and little bits of requirements and specifications.

Estimating the Business Value

You can use rational, analytical methods to assign business value to a story, of course. But another way is simple estimation. After all, if estimation is good for effort, why not use it for value?

The exercise described above add the TV show format to planning poker — I watch the show as *Dragon's Den* and most American readers will know it as *Shark Tank*, but it is also known as *Lion's Den* or *Money Tigers*.

The currency is a complete invention but adds some fun; combining a *wisdom-of-crowds* approach with a fantasy currency sidesteps the problems of using actual analysis and real money. Because the estimates are relative to each other, there is no claim of accuracy, only magnitude and ordering. And because the estimates come from intuition and gut feeling, the technique is quick and disputes are handled face to face.

In a classroom setting I normally divide participants into teams, but in a real-world setting one could draw each group from those in the company who have investment and product knowledge. Surprisingly, the conversations follow similar patterns regardless of who plays investors, experts or novices.

Typical developers know a lot more business language then many business people realise - they've seen the same shows! When asked to role-play as investors developers enjoy demonstrating their knowledge in questioning product owners about markets, opportunities and competitors.

While value estimates and priority are the most obvious outcomes from this process, it is perhaps the conversations and discussion the process encourages that can be the most interesting outcome. Put on the spot to pitch rather than deliver a dry business case, product owners become animated. Those playing investors are free from office etiquette to critique and criticise proposed products and stories because they are role-playing.

And everyone has fun.

It isn't necessary to value every card (although you could), because the entrepreneur team is making priority decisions as they go. Understandably, bigger, epic-type stories get bigger business valuations than smaller stories, so it perhaps makes sense to do this exercise early in the development before epics and stories get broken down in detail.

The Result: Prioritization and Conversation

These days I recommend every story have a value estimate attached before asking team members to assign effort estimates. The value estimate is good, but this technique also has other benefits. For a start, the conversation is incredible. The exercise is a form of war-gaming, with one side challenging the other. Assumptions get exposed, requirements expanded, specifications flushed out, opportunities identified, and stories junked.

At the end of the process the team has a first cut at prioritization simply by looking at the highest value. Of course, anyone can argue with the prioritization, but that discussion is itself valuable.

The spread of values makes it easy to slot another story into the sequence. And if something drops in value (priority), the whole backlog does not need renumbering.

More importantly, with a value written on the card in business points, teams can engage in meaningful cost-benefit analysis and trade-offs.

A couple of hours playing your own version of *Shark Tank* can be very educational.

12. Effects of Time on Value

A few years back I spoke with the head of business analysis in a division of a major US bank. "I don't want BAs doing any analysis until the system architects have suggested a solution," he said.

"But how do the architects know what is wanted?" I asked.

"Oh, they have a general idea from the requests," he replied, "but I don't have enough people to review every request; there are too many. If the architects look first, we can drop those that aren't doable or take too long. Then after they put effort estimates against them, the project managers will rule some out so there is less work for my people."

Naturally, the architects told me the same thing in reverse. Each side was attempting to limit its workload by making the other side take on the larger task. If every business worked this way, nothing would ever get done.

It's important to attach business benefit—preferably a quantifi-able value—to user stories, and the early chapter discussed on how you might go about doing this. Now, I want to turn our attention to how *time* affects our view of value.

Value before Estimates

Too often companies assign effort estimates to work before they ever consider value. (Even worse, many organizations never assign value to user stories at all.) Perhaps because effort estimates are relatively easy — "Just ask the developers" — it is common to find that effort estimates are the only criteria for deciding whether work is undertaken. Value takes a back seat because there is a constant demand for "quick wins" and getting the biggest bang for your buck. Although if you think about it, if you don't know the value of work how do you know how big the *bang* will be?

Placing only effort estimates on stories means story selection is usually based of minimum effort, or what fits within the time or budget remaining. Without understanding value, that "biggest bang" might not end up being so lucrative after all.

Things get really factious when developers point out how difficult it is to come up with a realistic estimate. Even in the absence of value estimates, business representatives are quick to say, "But how can we do cost benefit analysis without the cost?" The bottom line is you can only do cost-benefit analysis if you have estimate for both the cost and the benefit.

Even if you do consider both factors for analysis, I have observed that those who make work requests always attribute a benefit to their work requests that is greater than the cost. The problem is, making effort estimates before value estimates creates an anchor; if a business representative knows a story will take ten days to complete, then they will — consciously or subconsciously — place a value on the story that is greater than the cost of ten days of work.

An assessment of value needs to precede effort estimation. Adding value first allows benefit to become an engineering constraint; estimating value second means it will be anchored in the effort estimate.

Engineer within Constraints

When benefit analysis happens before technical design and effort estimates, the expected benefit forms a constraint for the proposed work. Engineers can apply their skills and knowledge to suggest solutions proportionate to the expected benefit.

Imagine a potential customer walks into your software engineering shop and says, "I want to set up an online store to sell the widgets I make. I believe I can turn over ten million dollars a year within three years and make a profit of at least a million dollars by year four."

Think of the solution you might suggest. Next, imagine another customer walks in and says, "I want to set up an online store to sell the widgets I make. I believe I can turn over one hundred thousand dollars a year within three years and make a small profit in year four. I hope to give up my day job eventually."

These are very different problems to an engineer. The expected benefit is a constraint on the proposed solution.

The Cost of Delay

Having a quantifiable benefit allows us to consider the cost of delay — the change in value of delivering a solution later. Features and deadlines are normally presented as binary: "Feature x must be complete by December 1." However, using value relative to time changes the request and adds context: "Delivering x by November 1 is worth some money; by December 1, a lot of money; and after January 1, no money."

While some stories do indeed become worthless when delivered late, such as delivering a Santa Claus app on January 1, others do not. Indeed, there is probably little difference in value between a Santa Claus app being delivered on September 1 versus on October 1. Delivery on November 1 probably represents some lost value, but value falls faster with every passing day, as you can see in the figure.

Cost of delay for delivering a Santa Claus app between September 1 and January 5

Attaching value to a story allows teams to discuss how that value might change over time. Adding that time dimension to value-based prioritization leads to some interesting results. For instance, imagine you have a high-value item with a low cost of delay and a low-value item with a high cost of delay. In this case, it makes sense to do the low-value item first because the value of the more valuable higher story will remain unchanged over time, while the lower-value item has a shorter shelf life. Completing the low-value item first allows you to maximize your value by getting both items done at their peak values.

Imagine your team is also developing a Halloween app at the same time as the Santa app. The next figure shows the value against time for this app.

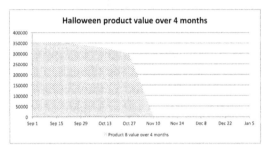

Cost of delay for delivering a Halloween app between 1 September 1 and January 5

Developing the Santa Claus app first makes it likely that all the value of the Halloween app will get lost. To maximize value overall, it makes sense to develop and release the Halloween app first, before starting work on the Santa Claus app.

The value from the Halloween app more than makes up for delivering the Santa Clause app a little later. But delivering either app too late destroys all value. If risk is the key driver, the team should not even attempt the Halloween app.

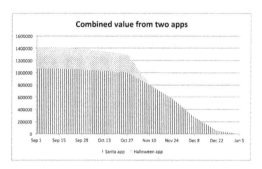

Delivering both apps maximises value

Obviously, one must know both value and how it changes over time to undertake such analysis. Don't be intimidated — perfect numbers aren't essential; estimates of the value are good enough. However cost-of-delay conversation without any number, even a random number, are usually too abstract to follow; far better to stick a number on a story and talk about how it can go up or down than just talk about how a number might change.

(For a complete discussion of cost of delay see Don Reinertsen's book *Principles of Product Development Flow*, 2009. While "cost of delay" is the industry term I find it misleading: to me *cost of delay* implies extra costs incurred because something is late, whereas the idea here is really "value lost" because of slower delivery.)

Time, Value, and Risk

Managing software work through effort alone is easy: Get a budget, do some estimates, and work to keep to both. But considering only these two factors can leave money on the table.

Managing through value is a game-changer, even if it is more difficult and requires more skill.

When you manage through costs alone, it is difficult to win arguments. There is always someone somewhere who will offer a lower price. But considering value — in particular, the effect of time on value — makes for more intelligent conversations and better decisions.

13. Maximising return on investment

Some people love to talk about return on investment; some people hate the idea. Either way, it's definitely a misunderstood subject.

Let's start from basics. Return on investment is often calculated simply:

$$ROI = \frac{Net\,Return}{Investment}$$

That is, the gain of an investment minus the cost of the investment, all divided by the amount invested. For example, if I invest $1 million in a software team and then receive $1.1 million, the net return is $100,000 and ROI is 10 percent.

$$ROI = \frac{\$1,100,000 - \$1,000,000}{\$1,000,000} = 0.1 = 10\%$$

Easy, right?

Well, not exactly.

More to Modeling and Calculating ROI

Other possible uses for the money play a part in the ROI calculation. If the same money could be nice and safe in a bank, earning, say, 5% a year, then ROI is really just 5% (10% minus the 5% a bank would pay). Risk plays a role, and the risk-free option provides a baseline against others are measured. After all, why spend money on a risky venture if the return isn't notably more than leaving the same money nice and safe in a bank?

Financial experts normally "discount" returns against a very safe investment, typically government bonds. So, any investment should represent a return greater than that which simply lending the money to Uncle Sam would make.

To complicate matters, although interest rates are often stated in annual terms, interest payments on savings accounts are usually made monthly. Thus, calculations should be modeled on a month-by-month base.

(To complicate matters further, there are different ways of modeling and calculating the return on investment. I'm sticking with NPV—net present value—here.)

Suppose a company invests $83,333 per month in a software development effort for a year—a total of $1 million. In the final month, the team delivers a product worth $1.1 million. Because some money was spent a whole year before the investment paid off, the calculation changes: The actual return is 7.3 percent, or $73,000 net.

So time can reduce the rate of return, simply spending the money later, let alone delivering the software sooner, will increase the return on investment. This in itself is an argument for developing software faster and delivering sooner — something I'm sure many developers are aware of.

But this logic also plays into the agile way of working. Consider again that development over twelve months. Imagine instead that the team made monthly releases and deliveries. That is $91,666 each month for twelve months. Now the return jumps to $97,300, or 9.73 percent. If delivery moves to weekly releases, the return sneaks up a bit further.

Value-Based Prioritization

Projects often can get stuffed with irrelevant additions. Perhaps some requirements are in there to ensure a particular executive agrees to the project. Leftover requirements from a previous project are probably there too, and some get added because people know how difficult it can be to get work in later.

Considering a project as a singular, whole, atomic, all-or-nothing endeavour prevents teams from streamlining work. Simply by cutting the low-value stories, teams can improve the project's ROI. Traditionally, a project gets treated as a collection of requirements forming a single unit — perhaps even a single delivery — directed at unlocking some business benefit. But giving individual stories value helps you prioritize and see where unnecessary work can be cut.

Once you apply cost of delay thinking, ROI calculations that respect time, and continuous delivery, the project model itself starts to break down. For example, suppose your team is working on a project and uses cost of delay and ROI to choose the work to do next from the project backlog and delivers it as soon as it is ready. After a while, if you simply work through the backlog in value order the value of the items being done will start to decline

Sticking with the original project requirements results in teams delivering less value per release as the project progresses. The highest-value stories get delivered early, leaving low-value stories for later releases. However, in practice, teams will embrace new requests through scope creep that generate more value, and thus deliver relevant, valuable work throughout the project's lifecycle but may never complete all the original requirements.

Next Stop: Continuous Delivery

The arguments about delivering in iterations are well established, but they tend to centre on feedback cycles—how releasing software earlier creates feedback and accommodates changing requirements better, and how such cycles reduce risk because teams can make corrections during development.

Focusing on feedback, changes, and risk reduction misses a more important element: **Regular deliveries can actually increase the value—the return on investment—from software.**

Forget whether agile or waterfall is right for some project or another; instead, ask whether you want to increase the ROI. There should be only one answer to that.

Return on investment increases simply because working software is delivered to customers and put to work sooner. Therefore benefits, possibly revenue and/or cost savings, from the investment are realised sooner. Of course releasing software sooner creates more opportunities for feedback - which may further increase the value of the software. And being good enough to release software early and regularly indicates not only that the development team are performing well but that they are keeping quality higher - if they weren't doing both of these things they simply wouldn't be able to deliver regularly. Consequently this approach also reduces risk.

For such a team continuous delivery becomes the obvious next step. Releasing software immediately after coding and testing is complete increases return on investment, minimizes the cost of delay, and accelerates feedback cycles. What's not to like?

Story by Story

Teams can boost ROI far higher if instead of considering the ROI on a project level, they consider value, ROI, and cost of delay on a story level. Projects are simply big bundles of requests (stories) that arrive at the same time. If you add value, ROI, and delay analysis to each story in the bundle, you can increase the value of work.

The challenge is to adopt new approaches that allow teams to think of work in small, individual pieces. This will require a mind shift, but it's worth it when you consider how much it can maximize project value.

14. Writing stories - where do I begin?

There is no one best place, time or way to start writing user stories and building up your backlog. In fact it is almost certain that there is some better time to start - maybe last week, and some better place to start - maybe when you understand what the overall aim of the work is, and almost certainly there are better techniques to use than you currently know.

Still, none of that is an argument for postponing making a start. Whenever and wherever you start is the right place to start.

1st Law of Backlogs: **You don't need a big backlog**.

In the beginning there only needs to be enough backlog to get the technical team started. There are reasons you might want to build up a bigger backlog but there are also reasons to avoid big backlogs. When getting started you only need enough to feed the technical team the next iteration.

Actually it probably makes sense to have slightly more backlog than you expect the team to do just in case you get lucky, or unlucky, and find more can be done than you expect, or something needs to be substituted.

In fact, you can extend this argument across the whole development period. When needs and understanding are changing rapidly there are good reasons for taking a just-in-time approach to story creation, However most product owners tend to build up more than enough backlog.

So, right at the start of a new initiative where and when should you start writing stories and start creating your backlog? There are several model answers to this question, one of which might, perhaps with modifications, match your situation.

Backlog?

A backlog is a collection of work to do. Scrum describe two backlogs: the sprint backlog, the work that will be done in the current iteration/sprint, and the product backlog: work which will be done in a future sprint.

Sprint backlogs are typically a small collection of user stories and tasks (where tasks are being used). Product backlogs are typically composed of user stories and epics (where epics are being used.)

Solo brainstorm

Suppose you are parachuted into a team as product owner. The team has just been formed, or might still be forming, the previous product owner left under a cloud and left no artefacts.

All you know about the initiative is the title of the work.

In this scenario you are racing against the clock. The team will want to start work, you might be able to buy a little time by telling the team they can "get ready" for a week or two - allow them to install some new servers, set up a CI server, create a CD pipeline and so on. However doing any work implies making assumptions about what is needed and what is to be built.

What you need to know is: *when is the first planning meeting?*

Once you know this you know how much time you have to create a backlog. At a minimum you will need a few hours, say half a day, of intensive thinking and writing to actually create the stories. You can do that immediately before the planning meeting. Now you know how long you have to do some analysis, investigation, to find stakeholders and talk to them,

Suppose your assignment starts 9am on Monday morning, the first planing meeting is 2pm on Thursday. You can use Thursday morning to pull your thoughts together and bang out some stories. That means you have Monday, Tuesday and Wednesday to do research.

Of course it would be better if you could start a week earlier but maybe that is not an option. It could also be worse, you might find the meeting is scheduled for 2pm on Monday.

Remember: that writing a story does not commit you to doing a story. You might bang out 20 possible stories in the few hours available and the team might accept five for development, those five might change during development and the other 15 might never be seen again.

2nd Law of Backlogs: **Stories in a backlogs are not guaranteed to be built**, they are possibilities.

Of course, it is always better to work with someone. Which brings us to the next option.

Group brainstorm

Another way to make a fast start is to just sit down with a group of interested parties - business users, programmers, testers, customers, whoever! - and talk about what the system will do and as you do write stories.

Such a meeting might be called a "Story writing workshop" and even a free format session should come up with some usable stories.

It helps to know what the overall aim, objective, goal or *Big Hairy Audacious Goal* (BHAG) of the work is. Knowing the ultimate objective can help guide story writing and act as a filter when reviewing possible stories.

Unfortunately such goals are often absent. Sometimes such goals only become apparent as the work unfolds. Fortunately the absence of a goal need not stop the work starting - although it might stop it from stopping! If you don't know the ultimate goal then one of the aims of the work should be to uncover the goal.

A more structured approach might start by calling out who all the interested parties are. Each of these can be written on an index card. This forms the initial stakeholder list.

Some of these stakeholders will actually use the system. You might mark all such stakeholders with an asterix if you are writing them on cards. These stakeholders are the users - a horrible term but on which is commonly used in our industry.

You can do quickly sort the roles into priority order. Take the top one and ask "What does this person do with the system?" The answers to this question can from User Stories. You might stick with these these stories and this role and "go deep" - writing out more actions and splitting the stories you have written into smaller ones.

If you can observe one of these users, or have one of them in the workshop, then good. Grab the opportunity, pull them into your meeting and ask them what they do. Ask the to describe a typical day at work, or tell you the problems they face.

Instead of going deep on a user roles you might decide to go broad and write a few stories for each the (key) roles you have identified. You might then double back and work some more on the stories which are likely to be built soon: add acceptance criteria, split the stories into multiple smaller stories and so on.

Such a workshop could go on for days and days but most likely half a day will give you more than enough stories to get the team started. You might choose to reconvene the workshop periodically to continue building the backlog when needed.

If you need to make a quick start then a simple workshop is probably the best option. When you have more time, or later when you double back to look again at your stores, then it might be time to try Story Mapping[1] or to apply a technique like Impact Mapping[2]. These can provide new insights into work, generate more ideas for stories or change the way you see existing stories.

A story writing workshop - especially one conducted under time

---

[1]User Story Mapping: Building Better Products Using Agile Software Design, Jeff Patton, 2014

[2]Impact Mapping, Gojko Adzic, 2012

pressure - may not be the best place to add acceptance criteria. When brainstorming you probably just want to hammer out ideas. At some later point you will want to add acceptance criteria, maybe in another group workshop but acceptance criteria can be added at other times, perhaps as an solo analysis exercise, or perhaps in discussion with actual users. In the acceptance criteria can be added during the planning meeting or as the first task once the story enters the sprint.

Write as you visit

The two options described so far should work when you need are pressed for time. They may also be used when more time is available or you might choose to take a more measured approach.

You might start with a rough stakeholder identification session. Using this initial list you can visit the stakeholders and ask about their expectations. As you interview them you may make notes which you use to write stories later on or you might write stories there and then.

One word of caution, whatever you do avoid giving the impression that anything you say or write represents a guarantee to build something - remember the second law of backlogs. It is very easy for stakeholders to behave like children dictating a list to Santa Claus, and as we all know, children have unrealistic expectations of what presents they will get.

Either way you will rapidly gather up stories. At some point you will want to look at your collection as a whole, find the duplicated, find the overlap and the contradictions. Again story mapping, impact mapping and more traditional analysis techniques can be applied later on. One shouldn't be fear these approaches increasing the work to do, they should also identify work which doesn't need doing.

Big requirements doc

The scenarios sketched so far assume little or no existing knowledge or artefacts. However it is more common to find the reverse situation: an excess of documentation.

Faced with volumes of documentation a new product owner has a quick decision to make: use or ignore it?

One of the problems with documentation is it decays over time. As documents get older the world around it changes, needs change, and the validity of the documents decays.

Another problem is that while people see documentation - especially requirements documents - as a store of knowledge they are an imperfect store. Much of the knowledge they should convey never leaves the head of the writer. So it may well be that documentation contains errors and omissions even before it starts its slow decay.

Yet another common problem with documentation is that is may well mix up solution and problem. It is not uncommon for "requirements" documents to make assumptions that imply a certain solution design, or even to make statements about the solution, e.g. "It should work like Microsoft Excel."

Finally it is also possible that voluminous documentation simply requires too long to read and comprehend.

So even when much preparatory work is present there may be good reason to makes some sympathetic noises about the usefulness of the tomes while ignoring them. In such a situation the product owner is back to the scenarios outlined already.

Alternatively, assuming useful, up to date, relevant, documentation the product owner's job is to start turning the requirements into usable stories for the development team. Feeding the development team the documentation on mass is likely to cause indigestion as the whole team slows to read everything.

In this scenario the product owner operates a metaphorical salami slicer. Their job to start slicing up the existing documentation into a series of stories which can be fed to the team. Again only enough needs slicing off to keep the team busy for the next iteration.

Work continues

The sections above set out several options for getting started on a backlog. Experiences analysts might well add their own preferred techniques for analysing the problem in hand and generating stories. Good! The above are not prescriptive or exclusive.

More tools and techniques can be applied in the beginning but more importantly they can be applied as work continues.

3rd Law of Backlogs: **Backlogs are never finished**

Backlogs will, and should, continue to grow, more stories will be added, others will be discarded and the rest will change over time.

It is also important for product owners to keep their understanding of what is needed fresh and up to date. This understanding should be reflected in the backlog and on the stories in the backlog.

Between planning meetings product owners have plenty of homework to do. They may well be working with the technical team, helping them understand stories they have taken into the sprint, perhaps helping with testing or perhaps reviewing work which is nearly done.

As a product owner no matter how you start you will need to keep applying techniques like these to keep loading the backlog. Backlogs should continue evolving during the duration of the work. You don't need to do it all at the start, you can add more later, you can change what you have and scared some.

Even if you have salami sliced an entire library of requirements documents to start with, or held a week long story writing workshop, and even if you have all the stories you think you could possibly need you still want to keep working the backlog.

You will want to keep doing your research on what is needed. You need to revisit stakeholders, see how their thinking and needs are changing, see what they think of what has been built so far and how that has changed their understanding of what is needed.

Backlogs will, intentionally or unintentionally, contain ideas which do not go forward to development. These need to be identified and removed - and the sooner the better!

When things are delivered product owners need to revisit those who made the original request and ask: How has this changed your work? What benefit has be created? Such evaluations can feed back into future stories and prioritisation.

You need to keep up with how the technology is changing and how that might have an effect on the work you are doing.

And you need to keep abreast of a myriad of the other things which might change your original understanding of need.

> 4th Law of Backlogs: **Backlogs are not comprehensive**, they do not contain all the work to be done.

> Backlogs do not, and should not, contain all the knowledge of what is wanted, nor do they contain all the knowledge needed to build the right system and they certainly don't contain all the detail on what is wanted.

> A User Story is a placeholder for a conversation, a token for work to be done; the necessary knowledge is in people's heads.

Homework pays off when it comes time to prioritise work, to review work and when the next planning meeting rolls round. Unless product owners do their homework and keep their knowledge fresh and up to date they may be able to go through the motions in a planning meeting but they will add little value.

15. Backlog structure

The requirements discovery process and the development creation process are normally buffered by one or more backlogs. Stories - or any other piece of work - sit in the backlog waiting for their turn in development.

There are those who would argue that backlogs should not exists. They have a point. Perhaps the ultimately metric of true Agility is the time it takes for an idea to move from "An idea" to a working, delivered, product in the hands of a customer. This is sometimes called "cycle time." Pursuit of short cycle times would lead teams to minimise time spent sitting in any backlog. And one way to eliminate time waiting in the backlog is simply to eliminate the backlog.

However backlogs can have their uses. One very basic use is levelling the flow of work into a team. This means reducing the peak demands by postponing some work, i.e. storing work in the busy times for quieter periods. A small backlog allows work to be moved from peak time to off-peak times.

A more common reason for having a backlog is simply that most organizations like to have some idea of what might be happening in future. Removing backlogs and "living in the moment" is not necessarily the best way to operate. But, sometimes this desire to know "what will happen" and "when will it be done" leads to backlogs which will take years to complete. This is rarely a good thing.

How the backlog is structured can make life easier, or harder, for those charged with managing the backlog. Structure can also play a part in shaping the attitude of the organisation to future work.

Two backlogs good

The classical Scrum model has two backlogs in the middle of the process: the *product backlog* and *sprint backlog* - also called the *iteration backlog*. These serve as temporary repositories.

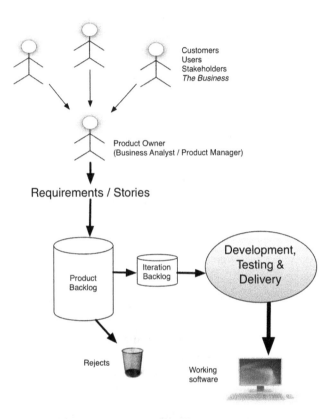

Simple model of product and iteration backlog

The product backlog contains all the items that might be developed for the product. These are typically written in User Story format and may be considered development stories in their own right or they might be *epics*, i.e. large stories which will be broken down into multiple smaller stories.

Product backlog stories should be meaningful and add value to end users (i.e. customer, or *the business*). As previously discussed each should carry a statement of business value, ideally a number but a statement of value might work too.

At the start of each iteration a few product backlog stories are selected from the product backlog for development in the next iteration. If helpful these are broken down into a number of work tasks. These stories and associated tasks then constitute the sprint (iteration) backlog.

The sprint backlog is the focus of the technical team's work during the iteration. In all likelihood some of the backlog items will remain undone at the end of the iteration.

Although in practice the requirements and technical activities are rarely as cut as this model implies. The degree to which they overlap varies.

The requirements engineers and product owners will work with the technical team during the iteration to answer questions about items from the sprint backlog. They may be involved in refining specifications and writing acceptance criteria, the need to sit with developers to mock up screens, or discuss details, and they may work with testers.

Product owners and requirements specialists will also be looking to the future. They will continue talking to stakeholders and customers, they will continue adding stories to the product backlog. They will also be refining, editing, changing items already in the backlog. Importantly they will also be thinking about that will be requested in the next iteration planning meeting.

Importantly, just because an item has been placed in the product backlog does not guarantee it will be delivered. The product owner needs to keep the backlog under review. Some items may be removed because they are no longer relevant, valuable or high priority.

Overtime the focus of requirements work will change, exactly how it changes depends on the environment the team is working in. Possibilities include:

- In a stable environment initial requirements work may focus on discovering requirements. Once the bulk of requirements are identified and placed in the backlog discovery slows and requirements engineers focus on specification and detail. In effect the requirements team switch from breath to depth.
- In a rapidly changing environment discovery work is ongoing. The team continuing gathering and refining requirements requests, and working to understand the business benefits. The focus of their work is controlling the demand for work and ensuring business benefits are maximised.

Three backlogs better

For teams working in iterations it makes complete sense to have an iteration backlog: a short list of all the work they aim to do this iteration (give or take a bit.) However the product backlog can be more troublesome.

One reoccurring problem with the product backlog is that it becomes full of good ideas for work which *could* get done. It becomes so full of work that it becomes difficult to think rationally about the work to do. As the old saying goes: "you can't see the wood for the trees."

Product backlogs naturally grow but that causes a problem for organizations which consider the end, "project finished," as being the completion of everything that was asked for. Product Owners are can be caught in a vicious circle, they feel the need to show how useful they are by adding to the backlog, but adding to the backlog takes them away from the delivery team who also need their knowledge. A growing backlog, or backlog that is not reducing as expected pushed the product owner to work hard, so they write more stories and the backlog grows.

A better model can be to use three backlogs:

- **Opportunity backlog**: all the ideas which have been suggested and have been considered worthwhile for recording.

  Recording such ideas does not in any way commit anybody to actually undertaking them. Ideas in this backlog may be crude, unrefined and in need of more investigation and refinement.

- **Validated backlog**: items from the opportunity backlog which have been examined, researched and discussed enough to be considered valid candidates for future development.

  Critically items in this backlog have been assessed for business benefits and the results recorded with the requirement.

- **Iteration/Sprint backlog**: as before, the work that will be attempted in the current iteration.

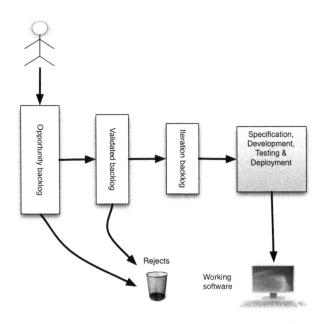

Three backlogs

While the iteration backlog plays the same role as it ever did - setting the agenda for the next iteration - splitting the product backlog allows for a clear separation of "good ideas" and "validated ideas." Moving from the former to the latter involves checking ideas with stakeholders, measuring them against the over-arching goal, considering the benefits in the market, or to the wider organization, and perhaps conducting experiments to measure benefits.

There are two criteria for moving items from the opportunity backlog to the validated backlog:

1. There must be space in the validated backlog: the validated backlog is deliberately limited in size.
2. Items in the validated backlog must have clearly identified business benefits, and hopefully estimates of business value, should be allowed to enter the validated backlog.

The name *validated* is chosen to mean: business benefit assessed and validated. If an item is moved from the opportunity backlog to the validated backlog without a business value being assigned then assigning a business value becomes an urgent task.

Rather than forward planning focusing on effort it should focus on value and benefits. Therefore no effort estimates should be placed on items in the opportunity backlog - after all many if these items will never progress any further.

Only items in the validated backlog may be estimated at terms of effort - there is no point in estimating effort for items in the opportunity backlog which may have no business benefit. By implication benefit or value estimation comes before effort estimation.

It is reasonable to consider all items in the opportunity backlog as if they are epics. When these items move from opportunity to validated then they need to be broken down into smaller stories. Similarly, when they move from the validated backlog to the iteration backlog they are broken down from stories to tasks.

The three backlogs correspond to three planning horizons:

- The iteration backlog is the near time, probably the next two weeks.
- The validated backlog is the medium term, probably no more than 12 weeks (3 months).
- The opportunity backlog is the longer term, this may represent work which will not be done for years.

Deciding which items to move forward, from opportunity to validated and from validated to iteration, it important work for product owners. This may require them to do research into an item before deciding to move it forward - or discard or even push back the the item.

When an item advances there is more work to do: fleshing out detail, breaking epics and stories down, possibly obtaining business value estimates or effort estimates. There is little point in doing work on items which are not moving forward, they can wait their turn, they may never be done.

Epics need not be broken down in their entirety before work is undertaken. Possibly the first stories broken out of any epic would be experiments which could test technology options and, more importantly, market and client reaction. For example the first stories for an epic entitled "Launch French version" might describe a series of data gathering experiments to assess the size of the market and opportunities. Translation, payment and such can wait, they might never need doing.

For the requirements specialists there is different work associated with each backlog:

- Items in the opportunity backlog need to be regularly reviewed, it is likely there will be far more items here than the team can look at in the near future. Some items will be reviewed and thrown away. Other items will be reviewed and further work postponed. A few items will be reviewed, then explored in detail and benefits assessed. After the benefit assessment the item may be moved to the validated backlog or it might be removed.

- Items in the validated backlog are likely to be done some-time in the next quarter. Any open questions need to be answered and details need to be understood before they are submitted for the iteration backlog.

- Items in the iteration backlog are in the process of being worked on by the delivery team. The requirements team need to be on hand to answer questions, clarify specifica-tions, resolve queries and generally keep the work moving.

While the Product Owners, BAs and others in the requirements team will work with the delivery team during the iteration to deliver the iteration backlog some time will be spent on the other two backlogs. A little time will be spent each iteration combing through the opportunity backlog, removing items with limited benefit and promoting others to the validated backlog. Indeed, one would expect most of time to be spent on items promotion candidates and ensuring validated items are ready to move forward.

Finally

Backlogs represent work which is not moving forward. Scrum style product backlogs in particular can become full of *work to do*. Work waiting in the backlog is work which is slow. Teams aiming for rapid delivery - from idea to deployment - may well want to eliminate backlogs altogether.

However for most teams having some buffer of work to do is beneficial. It allows for flow through the team to be managed, it allows incoming work to be prepared and it allows for forward planning.

The Scrum style two-backlog model is by far the most widely used however there are teams using a three backlog model very successfully. The keys to the three backlog model:

- Limited the work in the middle backlog, the validated backlog so it does not become an ever expanding list of work to do.
- Making business benefit/value the driving force behind each item of work and progress through the backlogs.

16. Alternatives

User Stories are far from being the only way of capturing work to be done. Many traditional requirements capture techniques are applicable whether the team is working Agile or not. The trick is, as always, to meet your need without incurring unnecessary costs and effort.

Any approach which is value but before you rush to dismiss user stories and embrace another approach consider these attributes of User Stories:

- User Stories are light weight: they don't impose a lot of (up front) costs on the team.
- They are easy to comprehend: you don't need a five day course to understand them.
- They are easy to share between technical team and customers.

For me it is the third of these attributes that make User Stories the best approach I know of to date. Many other techniques are superior in terms of analysis, rigour and completeness of the document. But these advantages come at a significant cost: these approaches form a barrier between those skilled in the approach (typically IT staff) and those who are not (typically customers and users.)

Take a standard like IEEE 830 "Recommended Practice for Software Requirements Specifications". Or rather don't, this standard was replaced by IEEE 29148. There is a lot to this standard, should we expect a customer to be familiar with the standard in order to read a document produced by a standard? (The real problem with requirements written to confirm to this standard is that they are incredibly boring to read, I defy anyone to read an IEEE complaint requirements document and stay awake!)

The more we add to requirements the more they become a barrier to communication between the technical team and the customer. The technical team may be well versed in their chosen approach but the customer won't be.

Introducing a specialist, say a Business Analyst, into the mix to work as a translator can help but it is not cost free. Introducing an extra step creates costs, increases the changes of misunderstanding and generally complicates things. The BA is now the expert in the chosen technique and must explain it to both sides.

Still, User Stories are not the only option, even if you team is an Agile team, there are others. If one of these techniques sounds like it might work better give it a try for a bit, see what happens and then decide whether to stick with it or try another.

Stories, PBIs, JBTD, etc. etc.

Originally *Extreme Programming* [1] described development *stories*, no format was given. The first few "agile" efforts I worked on used cards with free-format English language descriptions on them. Sometimes these were a few words like "Persist upload to database" and sometimes there were a lot of words.

---

[1] *Extreme Programming Explained*, Kent Beck, 2000

User Stories aren't mentioned in the Scrum Guide - or at least not the last time I checked. Instead the Scrum Guide talks of "Product Backlog Items" (PBIs). Others have talked about "Jobs to be done" (JTBD) and sometimes say "Anything that needs doing and ads value."

As a... I want to... So that... is a format, a language convention. You are free to use whatever format you like. It includes who, what, why which tend to be three very very useful things to know but you can use any format you like - and call it anything you like.

Use cases

If your team use Use Cases [2], and use them successfully, if all the team members are happy and proficient with Use Cases then don't feel you have to change to User Stories. In many ways Use Cases are superiors to User Stories.

However User Stories have two great advantages over Use Cases.

Firstly they are much easier to read and therefore understand and to write. Actually they are a bit too easy to write which may explain why there are so many bad User Stories in the world.

Because they are easy to create and understand you can shown to, and even written by, actual end users and customers. It takes time to learn to create and even understand Use Cases - and similar techniques. As a result they form a barrier between the technical team and the non-technical stakeholders.

---

[2] *Writing Effective Use Cases*, Alistair Cockburn, 2001

By being simple User Stories encourage interaction and collaboration.

This also points us at the second advantage of User Stores: there is less of a learning curve to use them. Even on technical teams which try to use Use Cases some of those on the team will not really be familiar with them, some will not have completed training on them, some will not understand the significance and interaction of Actors and Scenarios with the Use Case.

For a team which is not already using Use Case - or a similar approach - User Stories are a far quicker way to get started. It also makes it easier for everyone on the team to contribute.

Persona stories

William Hudson[3] has proposed using Persona Stories instead of User Stories. These stories are superficially similar, for example:

> Mary wants to create and account so she can order
> some goods

Basically persona stories miss off the "As a" from the front. However, in order to write persona stories the personas need defining in advance. While some may see this as an added burden others will see it as an advantage.

Hudson claims that writing stories in this fashion increases developer empathy and understanding and therefore leads to

---

[3] *User Stories don't help users*, William Hudson, 2013, ACM Interactions, November + December 2013

better conversations and end results. Personally I think he is right, a small change can make a big difference.

Finally

Although this book repeatedly talks about User Stories most of the ideas easily transfer to the other techniques just mentioned. The ideas may require some modification but most of the techniques will work just as well with Use Case, Personas Stories, Jobs to be Done, Product Backlog Items or just plain Stories.

User Stories are easy to write, it is perhaps because they are so easy to write that so little care and attention is often given to them. While easy to write they are far harder to "get right." In fact, the perfect User Story probably does not exist and never will.

17. Last words of advice

This book has covered far more ground than I ever thought it would. So before closing let me return to the subject of User Stories and give some final words of advice.

Keep them Short

Originally teams used small index cards to capture development stories and User Stories. The idea was to deliberately limit the space. The limiting the space meant it was impossible to write a traditional requirement or specification, people needed to be concise, and needed conversations in addition to stories because the details were absent.

With the advent of electronic management tools (Jira, Rally, etc.) this constraint has gone. User Stories can be as long as you like. This is a disadvantage, not an advantage.

Keep stories short and avoid unnecessary words, details and boiler plate. Remember the old Agile adage:

"Do slightly less than you think is needed."

Break, don't bend, the format

If you find the story you want to write doesn't really fit in the "As a ... I want to ... So that ..." type format, and if squeezing it into that format makes for bad or difficult to read English then don't do it!

The Who, What, Why elements of User Stories are really useful so try and include these three points but don't feel you need to stick religiously to "As a ... I want to ... So that ..."

Write the story that makes sense in what ever format you like. In an environment where User Stories truly are tokens for work to be done and placeholders for a conversation then much of the advice about story format and style can be safely ignored. Remember the words of George Orwell:

> "Break any of these rules sooner than saying anything outright barbarous."

So that

If you can't come up with a genuine "So that" then just drop the clause altogether. Readers will recognise a contrived motivation clause and it will undermine the legitimacy of the story - and perhaps the writer.

Equally if the reason for doing the action is obvious then leave it out. There is no reason to use words on something which is either obvious.

However if you find that most of your stories omit the "so that" clause then it is time to consider again if the think you are building really does deliver benefit and whether the benefit could be realised in another, better, way.

Context is important

Because User Stories are placeholders for conversations, and because the interpretation of the story and the nature of the conversation depend on what participants know, then all stories are context dependent.

Unlike traditional requirements documents and analysis techniques User Stories do not try to capture all the details. Brevity is valuable, details are deferred.

If you pick up a random selection of User Stories it is easy to critique them and find anomalies and things which aren't clear. Only when one knows the context, indeed only when one lives the context, is it possible to decide if a User Story is good or bad.

That is not to say that context forgives all omissions and anomalies. Of course there are good and bad User Stories but to understand the story really requires understanding the space it was written in and will be read in.

Not an analysis technique

User Stories, unlike Use Case, are not an analysis technique. They were never intended to be an analysis technique and one should not think of them as an analysis technique.

The requirements engineering community - and I include the Business Analysis and Product Management professions here - have plenty of analysis tools to choose from if you need some tools.

In this aspect User Stories differ from Use Case: Use Cases
are as much an analysis technique as they are statements of
requirement or specification. User Stories are not, professionals
need to supplement User Stories with appropriate tools and
techniques.

Appendix: Requirements and Specifications

For many, perhaps most, development teams the terms *requirement* and *specification* are used interchangeably with no detrimental effect. In everyday development conversations the terms are used synonymously, one is as likely to ask for the "spec" as the "requirements."

However it is sometimes useful, and occasionally important, to differentiate between the two terms:

> "A requirement is a desired relationship among phenomena of the environment of a system, to be brought about by the hardware/software machine that will be constructed and installed in the environment. A specification describes machine behaviour sufficient to achieve the requirement. A specification is a restricted kind of requirement" (Jackson and Zave, 1995)

The key points to note are in the last two sentences:

- A specification describes behaviour to achieve requirement.
- Specification is a restricted requirement, i.e. the specification narrows down the requirement.

For example: there may be a *requirement* to store customers details for shipping and future marketing. The *specification* would state what details should be stored, e.g. name, postal address, e-mail address, etc. Specifications can be very detailed, e.g. a postal address should contain an house number or name, a street, a post code, and the format the post code should satisfy.

Specifications

In creating the specification the requirement may change. For example: should the system accept US style zip codes as well as UK style postal code? This depends on whether the system is required to service only UK customers. Consequently those commissioning the system might need to consider their international approach.

In exposing the detail of the specification the requirement may be brought into question, refined and even changed. A question of detail may ripple all the way up to the strategic level. Although, as with good code, one hopes that such ripples will not occur that often. If questions arising from specifications regularly ripple back to it may be a sign that the requirements, encapsulations or even strategy and goals are weak.

There is almost no limit to the detail a specification can reach. In University I was taught to write incredibly detailed specifications in formal, mathematical, logical notation called VDM-SL (Jones, 1986). Yet for many teams this level of detail is unnecessary and for most teams is not economically justified.

For many teams the specifications are uncovered as part of the coding process. Indeed code itself represents the ultimate specification of what happens. Unfortunately in code form the specification is difficult for non-programmers to understand and therefore agree to and, more importantly, verify.

Code is not a very useful mechanism for communicating between customers/users and programmers. Nor are formal specifications written in predicate logic good at promoting shared understanding. Like code formal specifications require readers to understand the notation, since customers rarely understand predicate logic, or code, these form creates a barrier between technical staff and non-technical customers.

In some fields leaving the specification to the programmers is a good thing. Programmers who understand the field may have little need of additional (expensive) documentation; in fast changing environments writing down a specification and communicating may injected undesirable delays.

In other fields it is preferable to have the specification understood in advance or determined by specialists. Competing organizations sometimes agree on specifications so that completing products to interoperate. For example, passing short SMS text message between competing handsets over competing networks using competing switching equipment requires all parties to follow agreed specifications.

For teams working in a traditional fashion - upfront requirements, specification and design - specifications can become a battleground. Programmers put under pressure, without knowledge or specifications, inevitably do things the consuming clients do not expect. One side or other will demand more detail next time to prevent the problem.

But more detail doesn't solve the problem because a) nobody

remembers the details, b) omissions and mistakes are made in specifying the detail, c) more detail leads to more things that can change, more things to be read (and forgotten) and more opportunities for mistakes in the detail. And d), excessive amounts or detail of specifications creates more of a barrier between the interested parties and therefore reduces the changes of finding misunderstandings.

Since the amount of detail is almost infinite the call "for more detail" easily escalates into an arms-race. Introducing more detail in specifications can quickly make things worse not better.

An example

Consider the CEO of a large super market change. His strategy is for increased market share. He, and his board, are prepared to trade profits for market share. The requirement he gives his COO is: increase sales.

Given this requirement the COO convenes his team. They determine that some B2G1F (Buy two get one free) offers are called for. They task the marketing team with deciding which products to apply the offers to and the IT team with providing the systems to implement this.

The IT team receive the B2G1F requirement and quickly realise that one requirement is for the products it applies to must be configurable. But how configurable? Does the marketing team require a web interface? Or can it be managed through a XML config file? The original requirement expands into multiple small requirements.

Then there is a question of how the offer is implemented. Requirements can become very specific. Obviously when a customer buys two identical products a third identical product is free. But what if the customer buys two of the products in large and a third small one? Is the third small? Or one of the large?

And when the marketing team say "1 litre fruit juices" does that mean that someone buying 1 litre each of orange juice, apple juice and cranberry juice gets one free? And does that mean the B2G1F offer needs to be marketed differently?

Requirements can be large, they can be small, they can hide details which later become significant. Over time requirements are refined, they are atomised and details added. At some point a requirement becomes a specification.

Enter the Iteration

When working in short iterations requirements are best given at the start of each iteration - not all requirements need to be known in advance but enough for the duration of the iteration should be.

(Teams which embrace unplanned work can happily start an iteration with missing requirements or respond to unexpected requirements. Teams which aim for maximum predictability will see unplanned work as problematic and aim to pin requirements down in advance.)

Specifications on the other hand might be known in advance or might be discovered during the iteration, either as a specific exercise or as part of the coding activity. Sometime leaving programmers to finalise specification is not only possible but advantageous. Other times specifications might be determined in advance by a specialist, typically an analyst of some description.

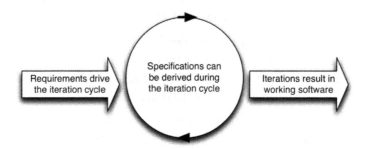

Requirements go in, working software comes out

Problems occur when specification are decided far in advance. When this is done specifications decay because:

- A changing world leads to specifications, and requirements, changing too.
- As the development team create the system they learn about both problem and solution domain, this can lead them to new insights.
- Without a deadline analysis can continue almost indefinitely, allowing more time for work to occur most likely leads to more work.
- The more specifications are decided the more that can change.
- Pre-emptively creating specifications will increase the amount of work done which is later discarded. Delaying specification creation reduces the chances that development work

is cancelled, removed or changes after specifications are created.

One source puts the rate of requirements and specification change at 2% per month (Jones, 2008), which works out at an annual compound rate close to 27%. Changed requirements means changes specifications which leads to rework.

Therefore it is preferable to decide specifications as late in the day as possible - say in the same sprint as coding will occur, or in the previous sprint. In the early descriptions of Behaviour Driven Development (BDD) Dan North described a Business Analyst working at the same keyboard as a programmer writing specifications as code was written.

And tests

A development story, especially when in *User Story* format (Cohn, 2004), is usually a requirement. It is a token for work to be done and is often called *a placeholder for a conversation*. The acceptance criteria often found on the back of a story card are specification but rarely are they a complete specification. Detail can be pinned down later in a conversation.

In some teams a fuller specification will be created in the form of acceptance criteria produced by a requirements engineer or professional tester before coding begins. If this is not done then the specification will be completed at the time of coding or at the time of testing.

Differences in interpretation of requirements and specification by programmers and testers is a common source of bugs. Two individuals read the same document, the programmer interprets it one way and writes code as such; the professional tester interprets it differently and tests it as such.

Formal methods removed this problem by using exact logical notation but in doing so make the specifications difficult for novices to read and increase the chances of errors in the specification itself.

Another solution is to use acceptance test scripts derived from acceptance criteria as the most detail form of specification. When these are written in natural language there is room for ambiguity. When written in a formal form ambiguity is squeezed from the system. When the formal form is executable - such as a FIT table or Gerkin *given when then* then it is possible to ensure the program code and specification match. This is an executable specification and further squeezes ambiguity from the process.

Whether in a logic based notation such as VDM-SL or pseudo-English Gerkin the aim is the same: a specification that can be executed by a machine. When this happens the code and specification match. The difference between the two approaches is in timing:

- Gerkin style executable specifications run after code is written as tests to ensure the human programmer produces the right thing. Such specifications highlight any differences so they may be eliminated.
- Logic based formal specifications aim to direct the code itself, either by executing the logic directly or by machine translation to a language such as C. Such specifications aim to stop any differences from ever occurring.

Although ambiguity may be squeezed out of specifications by formalising them it is more difficult to eliminate omissions. Continuing the earlier example, tests may be used to ensure an address postcode matches the prescribed format but tests cannot ensure customers supply their county, human intervention is required to ensure a specify county must be selected.

How much detail specifications and tests need to specify, and the point at which the details are decided varies greatly. For some teams specification can be left in the hands of the programmer when they are coding. In other environments specifications needed to be pinned down by specialists well in advance.

Whenever specifications and tests are to be used they should be created before coding begins. Creating them after the programmer has completed their work is to invite discrepancies and rework. While there is no guaranteed of eliminating all problems this approach can significantly reduce them.

Automated acceptance tests: the new formal methods

Automated acceptance tests, also known as executable specifications, continue the tradition of formal logic specifications. The tests are a specification. Automation demands formalisation because automation requires code. The first difference is that Gerkin style *given when then* specifications, for example, are readable by most people while VDM-SL predicate logic is only meaningful to those with years of experience.

It is interesting to note that the *give when then* specification format mirrors the pre and post conditions used in formal languages like VDM-SL. The *given* declares a set of pre-conditions and the *then* declares the post-conditions.

Secondly both techniques require tool support to be effective. But while predicate logic specifications tools are few and far between, expensive and difficult to use the tools used for executable specification are largely available free of charge as open source, e.g. Selenium, JBehave, Cucumber and FIT/FITNESSE.

Rather than providing a logical description of the program under development (as VDM-SL, Z, CSP and other formal methods do) these tools work through examples. Specifications are given by way of examples - hence the name *specification by example.* Because these examples are executable as tests it is possible to validate the program satisfies these specifications.

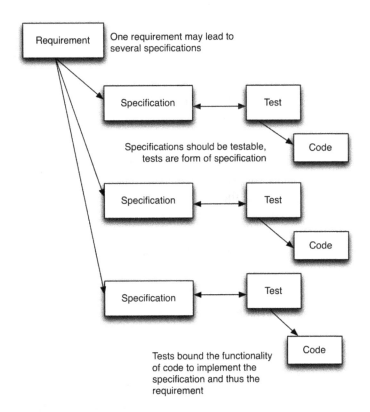

Requirements go in, working software comes out

These examples may not be exhaustive, there may be undefined behaviour in the system where specification examples are not provided. The program code is still the ultimate specification, the examples aim to cover observable behaviour where it is of significance to those doing the specification. (This differs from predicate logic descriptions which aim to be complete).

Because BDD and ATDD tests are machine executable they are

actually a form of formal specification. This author believes a useful line of research would be to see if such tests could be transformed in more traditional logical notations like VDM and Z

Knowledge and Trust

Whether specifications are needed or not often boils down to knowledge and trust. When developers have extensive knowledge of the domain they are working in then much of the information that would be contained in specifications already exists inside their heads. And when they have ready access to others who know more about the domain a verbal conversation may substitute for a written document.

For example, while most programmers will be familiar with the postal address example given previously, only those who work in specialist domains will know other formats. English legal practitioners frequently use DX mail rather than Royal Mail. A programmers who has worked in legal software for some years may automatically provide DX number and exchange in software while those new to the field need to be told, i.e. they need to given a specification, this may be written or verbal.

However knowledge alone may not be enough if programmers and testers are not trusted to use their own knowledge, or not able to ask for assistance when they recognise they do not.

Forgoing specification documents saves money because documentation is expensive. It also accelerates development because writing documentation is a time consuming process prone to blocking. Having a programmer determine specification as they code is the ultimate in just-in-time working.

Still there may be merit in having another person bring their knowledge and understanding to the specification effort. If these specifications are to match the code they must be created in some fashion which minimise opportunities for differences in understanding to emerge.

On anything other than trivial systems using human effort to validate that specifications and program match becomes a time consuming and error prone exercise, and thus slow and financially expensive. To overcome this specifications need to be both machine readable and executable - through automated tests or theorem validation - to ensure code and test specification say the same thing.

When knowledge and trust are lacking specifications become necessary, so too does an effective, usually automated, means of validating code against specification.

30 years ago the software industry attempted to solve the specification problem with formal methods. The BDD and ATDD techniques in use today take a similar approach but with a far lower barrier to entry. They in effect reinvent formal specification.

Conclusion

- There is often little point in differentiating between *Requirements* and *Specification* and the two terms are often used to mean the same thing, i.e. the thing to be built.
- Distinguishing between specifications and requirements can add to understanding.

- Requirements are best given at the start of each iteration but specifications can be discovered within the iteration. Finalising specifications as late as possible has a number of advantages.
- Requirements are unavoidably imprecise. Specifications should not be.
- Discovering specifications can lead to changes in the requirements. Requirements come before specifications but specifications can send ripples back to requirements.
- Specifications are test criteria; both specifications and test criteria can be formalised. Formalising specifications as predicate logic is time consuming and rarely justified. Formalising tests as executable specifications can be highly effective.

References

Cohn, M. 2004. *User Stories Applied*, Addison-Wesley.

Jackson, M. & Zave, P. 1995. Deriving specifications from requirements: an example. *Proceedings of the 17th international conference on Software engineering.* Seattle, Washington, United States: ACM.

Jones, C. 2008. *Applied Software Measurement*, McGraw Hill.

Jones, C. B. 1986. *Systematic Software Development using VDM.*

First published in Methods & Tools (http://www.methodsandtools.com/), Fall 2014 issue

Quick User Stories FAQ

What is the right size for a User Story?

There is no universal "right" size for a User Story. There is no "right" number of words, no right length of work, or "right" business value. All will depend on the team and concerns of your environment.

Each story should be deliverable in a short space of time, anything that takes more than two weeks is probably too big but there are teams that would regard anything that takes more than two days as too big.

In general the more a team know about the thing under construction - the more they know about the domain, the customers, the business model, etc. - the fewer words needed and the "larger" the request can be. That is, if the team know little about the domain, have never met a customer and work for a supplier company in another country the product owner will need to invest more time and detail in both the user story and the subsequent conversation.

Under such circumstances - and particularly when the technical team is in a different location - there can be pressure to write bigger stories. The development team may ask for more information, in writing. The product owners peers and superiors may suggest adding more detail. Under such circumstances writing more can be self defeating, the product owner spends more time writing so has less time for conversation, the development team are more restrained about asking questions and superiors think having everything in writing provides some sort of guarantee.

Remember: the longer a document, or story, is, the less likely it is to be read. And, the longer a document, or story, is, if it is read then the less the reader will remember.

At the other extreme, when the development team is in-house, when the team have been working in the domain for some years and have met customers then the product owner can express larger ideas in few words because the team know the context. Plus, the conversation which accompanies the user story will be better informed and, hopefully, shorter.

When is the conversation?

User Stories are often described as "A placeholder for a conversation" which begs the question, *when does the conversation happen?*

The conversation is not necessarily a single event. The conversation is an on going dialogue.

The conversation may start before the planning meeting, perhaps in a pre-planning meeting, it may later resume in the planning meeting, and again later on during development. Testers and coders - and anyone one else! - should ask questions of the product owner, customers, users, and others as they need to.

The conversation isn't over until the story is finished.

How do I determine business value?

There are several techniques, one or more may be appropriate:

1. Ask the stakeholders: even if they can't give a number in a currency ask them to give a statement.
2. Do analysis of what the organization stands to gain from the story: perhaps new revenue, perhaps cost savings, perhaps an improvement in quality, which may, or may not translate to a financial gain later. Take the analysis and construct a financial model - this may not be complicated although it might need to be.
3. Estimate the value: you might make an estimate based on your own analysis, an educated guess.

Or you might consult others: perhaps in a "delphic" approach by asking stakeholders and knowledgeable experts what value they think a story will deliver.

Or perhaps in a "wisdom of crowds" approach, I like to play "value poker" similar to the better known "planning poker" used for effort estimates. (See the *Estimating Business Value* chapter in *Little Book of User Stories*.)

How do I make my User Stories smaller?

Again there is no one right way of splitting stories. The following techniques often help:

1. Look at every conjunction (AND, OR, BUT) and split the story into two, one before the conjunction and one after.
2. Refine the roles and write more specific versions of the same story about each role.
3. Meet a few real life users who fill your roles then develop *personas* for the key roles. Rewrite the stories using personas and take the opportunity to split them.
4. Look at the value of the story and consider how you may realise some of that value with a subset of the story
5. If they story doesn't have any acceptance criteria write some.
6. Consider the acceptance criteria: see if you can make a separate story each acceptance criteria. You may end up with a basic version of the story and several stories which follow to add the original acceptance criteria. Some of the stories derived from the acceptance criteria might stand alone, others might be dropped altogether.
7. Create a story map and see if you can split out smaller journeys.
8. Talk to others! Get other opinions, the technical team can bring more eyeballs and brains to the problem. So too can other stakeholders and peers.
9. Show the stories to actual customers and users and talk see if they have insights which can make the stories smaller, or change the acceptance criteria.
10. Consider the story fidelity: could you write lower fidelity "dirt road" version?
11. If the technical team are breaking the story down to tasks then maybe some of the tasks could be stories in their own right? Or maybe some of the tasks could, with a

little tweak, be made into stand alone stories which have business value.

12. Repeat: writing user stories, and splitting them, isn't a one off activity. Revisit the stories on a regular basis and review them, ideally with someone else, and see if your thinking has changed.

This is not an exhaustive list by any means.

Remember: it is better to have more smaller stories than fewer bigger stories. But each story should deliver some business benefit (money, risk reduction, learning or something else) that the wider business can associate with.

When do I use a Story and when do I use and Epic?

Epics are placeholders for lots of stories. Epics will be broken down later into multiple stories. When that happens the Epic might exist as a "collecting" point or it might be removed all together - the stories need not have a common ancestor to be grouped (paper clips and rubber bands work too.)

Like stories an epic creates business benefit. It is even more important that epics deliver business benefit. The whole of an epics may deliver more value than the sum of the parts (the stories.)

Unlike stories epics cannot be delivered in less than two weeks. The large benefits they promise usually mean work will span multiple sprints and will be delivered a series of stories - each story will deliver some of the benefit although the whole (the epic) might be worth more than the sum of the parts (the stories.)

On the other side many teams break stories down to tasks. Tasks can be delivered very soon, days or hours but they do not normally deliver business benefit.

Epics are stories which deliver business benefits but are too large to be delivered quickly.

Tasks are mini-stories which can be delivered quickly but do not deliver business benefit. (Tasks are not normally written in User Story *As a...* format.)

Many teams don't use epics at all, and some teams don't use tasks. Most teams use two of the three available levels.

Finally, resist the urge to break epics down early. It is best to delay breaking the epics down until near the time when they are to be developed. Certainly there is little point in breaking an epic down which will not be done in the next three months. Any breakdown may well change during that time.

When epics are broken down it may be possible to delay developing some stories later. Indeed, some stories which originate in an epic breakdown may never be developed. If an epic breaks down to three stories and after the first two are built and delivered everyone is happy then why build the third?

How big should my backlog be before we start coding?

Big enough to keep the team busy for the coming iteration.

Big is not good for backlogs, small backlogs have many advantages: they are easier to manage, easier to reason about and keep overall cycle time low.

Some product owners want their backlog to include everything that might be done - something people forecasting an "end date" may well want know. Enlighten product owners recognise that no backlog can ever be complete and allow the backlog to evolve over time.

How do I write strong User Stories?

Practice.

Make sure the role in the story is real. Understand the role, perhaps add a persona.

Understand in detail how the customer will use the story. Understand how the story adds value.

Read other people's stories, have other people critique your stories.

But don't expect any story, no matter how strong to substitute for a conversation.

When is a User Story ready to go to development?

Now.

A story can enter development at any time if it is high enough priority.

It may be helpful to do some analysis on a story before development begins. It might be worth writing acceptance criteria for the story before it enters a development sprint. Some teams will place a value estimate and/or an effort estimate on the story in advance.

All of these things can make doing the story easier, perhaps faster, once it enters a development iteration but they are should not block work beginning. If any of this pre-work is need but not complete when a story enters an iteration then the work can be undertaken as part of the iteration.

For example, a team might write acceptance criteria for stories before accepting them into an iteration. However if an urgent story arrives the lack of acceptance criteria should not prevent the story from being scheduled into the iteration. If this happens then the first task in the iteration is for the acceptance criteria to be written.

Moving preparatory work on a story into the development iteration itself has several advantages: it minimises the chances that something changes between pre-work and development, it minimises the possibility that pre-work is undertaken for a story that is then cancelled, it allows the total amount of work on the story to be seen as part of the iteration.

That said many teams will set their own criteria for pre-work to be completed before a story enters an iteration. Therefore a complete answer to this question requires the asker to enquire into their working practices.

Acknowledgements and history

Many times I have looked at Mike Cohn's book (User Stories Applied) and thought "How can anyone get 200 pages out of User Stories?" They are simple, how much can you write about them?

Teams do find User Stories useful, they are a easy way to capture requests and contain three vital pieces of information: Who, What and Why. That is the obvious bit, the secret of User Stories is not the format, we could easily come up with another format, but the fact that they are easy to understand. Because they are easy to understand they help communication between all parties.

In the old days, before Agile, traditional requirements documents aimed to capture what was wanted and to promote co-operation between different groups (e.g. programmers, testers, customers, business sponsors) but, and this is a big but, because traditional documents were written in a very boring language ("The system shall...") or very precise language - sometimes even predicate logic - these documents actually formed a barrier between technical and non-technical staff working together.

Over the years I found myself helping more and more teams using User Stories. And I found that I kept giving the same, or at least very similar, advice again and again. After a while I started to think "I should write this advice down" but there was always something more important to write - most recently Xanpan.

The more I gave the same advice the more I wanted to write it down. Then in May 2015 I had a flight from London to Dallas. This was my opportunity, nine hours in the air with nothing to do. Shortly after take-off my laptop came out and I started. I don't know what the other passengers thought of me, tapping away furiously on my machine but I know that hours later when I came to put the machine away there I had 10,000 words. Far more than I expected.

I surprised myself not only that I had so much to say about user stories but that there was just so much to say about them! This also presented me with a problem.

10,000 words is a lot but it is not a book - not a traditional book anyway. Yet it is still far too big to be a magazine or journal article. Even the most generous online journals won't publish more than a few thousand at a time.

It was even too big to edit.

So I sat on it and wondered.

Then I remembered Johanna Rothman and the Agile Connection[1] online journal. Johanna had published a few of my pieces in the past and had offered to publish more. Maybe I could serialise the material?

Johanna jumped at the chance. But she also set me three constraints. First, as with previous articles she wanted each piece to be at most 1200 words. OK, a challenge but I can do that.

Second she asked me to add some stories, not user stories, war stories. Arh, I had one or two but I wasn't sure I could meet this.

---

[1]https://www.agileconnection.com/

I could see how readers would like it - after all, how many news paper stories start "Joe Smith was sitting back in his big arm chair remembering the day..." ? But could I do it?

I decided to wing it, that is an English expression meaning: chance it, improvise, make it up as I go along. With a little luck Johanna would forget this request quickly.

To my surprise once I started trying to think of stories I had them! Some of them may need rough edges knocking off, and the odd one might even be embellished a little to make a point clear but I had them!

Third, Johanna asked me to write in "the active voice." This was potentially the biggest challenge. I don't know what active voice it. Or rather, I can read a definition, I can read a contrast with passive voice and I can understand it for two minutes. But please don't ask me again. If you do I need to look up the definition again. To me its like those adjectives, verbs, noun things, o and the pronouns, prepositions and the rest. I don't know what they are and even when I learn I forget fast. In fact you can say that about English grammar altogether. As I tell my wife: I don't do grammar, I just write.

When I was learning to read and write the English education system didn't care much about grammar. In fact, they didn't care much about English. I was originally taught to read and write something called ITA. A seriously bad idea. Eventually my dyslexia came through and I spent four years out of mainstream school learning to read and write all over again, twice, actually.

So active voice was a big challenge. Luckily Johanna pointed me at a plugin for TextMate which highlighted all passive voice (its something to do with using words ending in "ed" or prefixed with "be".).

All in all I owe a big debt to Johanna. Since I started feeling the need to express myself I've been lucky enough to find people who have challenged me, and mediums which forced me to change. John Merrells as editor of ACCU Overload originally encouraged me to write and I developed a certain energy with writing. Blogging forced me to change and then writing patterns and attending pattern conferences helped me improve massively. Now Johanna and serialisation have challenged me again and initiated change, hopefully for the better!

So a big thanks to Johanna. A big thanks too to Beth Romanik of Agile Connection for copy editing my pieces, fixing the remaining voice, grammar, Americanising my English and getting the things online.

Not all the material here appeared in *Agile Connection*, the appendix, *Requirements and Specifications* originally appeared *Methods and Tools* as "Something Old, Something New: Requirements and Specifications" in the Fall 2014 issue. Many thanks to Franco Martinig, the M&T editor, for carrying this piece and many others.

Finally, the magic of LeanPub. Do you know using LeanPub you can accidentally write a book? Xanpan was an accident. As the User Stories pieces mounted up it became obvious they we ripe for recycling in a book. This is it.

allan kelly

September 2015

History

1.0 November 2015 - First chapters published

1.1 November 2015 - Chapters 3 (Assessing value) and 4 (Who) added

...

1.9 April 2016 - Added chapters 11, 16, 17: Estimating Business Value, Alternatives and Last Words of Advice

1.10 May 2016 - Added chapter 12: Time Effect

1.11 May 2016 - Added chapter 13: Maximising return on investment

1.12 September 2016 - Added FAQ to appendix and a new cover page

1.13 March 2017 - Allocated ISBN

Release 1.11 completes the initial book. All the Agile Connection material is included plus some new material and an appendix published in Methods and Tools.

During the course of creating the book to this point it has become clear that some other topics should be included. These may be added at a later date but for not the first edition is complete.